Metaphors the Church Lives By

Langham
GLOBAL LIBRARY

Metaphors the Church Lives By

Rethinking Church in the 21st Century

General Editors
Riad Kassis and Mark Labberton

Volume Editor
Elizabeth Sendek

Series Editor
Joshua Barron

Langham
GLOBAL LIBRARY

© 2025 Elizabeth Sendek

Published 2025 by Langham Global Library
An imprint of Langham Publishing
www.langhampublishing.org

Langham Publishing and its imprints are a ministry of Langham Partnership

Langham Partnership
PO Box 296, Carlisle, Cumbria, CA3 9WZ, UK
www.langham.org

ISBNs:
978-1-78641-101-3 Print
978-1-78641-140-2 ePub
978-1-78641-141-9 PDF

Scripture quotations in chapter 1, 5, and 6, and elsewhere marked (NIV) are taken from the Holy Bible, New International Version®, NIV®. Copyright © 1973, 1978, 1984, 2011 by Biblica, Inc.™ Used by permission of Zondervan.

Scripture quotations in chapter 2, and elsewhere marked (ESV) are taken from The Holy Bible, English Standard Version®, copyright © 2001 by Crossway, a publishing ministry of Good News Publishers. Used by permission. All rights reserved.

Scripture quotations in chapter 3, and elsewhere marked (NLT) are taken from the Holy Bible, New Living Translation, copyright © 1996, 2004, 2007, 2013, 2015 by Tyndale House Foundation. Used by permission of Tyndale House Publishers, Inc., Carol Stream, Illinois 60188. All rights reserved.

Scripture quotations in chapter 4 and 7, and elsewhere marked (NRSV) are taken from the New Revised Standard Version Bible, copyright © 1989 National Council of the Churches of Christ in the United States of America. Used by permission. All rights reserved.

British Library Cataloguing-in-Publication Data
A catalogue record for this book is available from the British Library

ISBN: 978-1-78641-101-3

Cover & Book Design: projectluz.com
Illustrations © Antonina Szczerba

Contents

Series Introduction

God's love in Jesus Christ for the salvation and recreation of all things is still the hope of the world. This Christian affirmation is the reality that "holds all things" and "holds all things together." Over the millennia of the biblical narrative, the God revealed in Scripture is present and active to a world in all its glories and agonies, in both personal and collective stories. In seasons when the people of God have flourished in God's faithfulness or doubted, even fought, God's intentions and desires, still God is faithful. The church belongs to its loving, healing, and renewing Saviour and Lord, Jesus Christ. Nothing will separate us from the love of God and even the gates of hell will not prevail against the church.

And yet the church is always a very mixed picture. Great reasons exist for the vitality, truthfulness, and love of Christian communities. Right alongside are all the doubts and insults hurled against God because of the church – from inside and outside – which have been and are profuse. Generation by generation, the church has struggled to discern and practice its spiritual and theological identity in real time and in real places. As we look at the church around the globe today, we give thanks for faithful Christians, often in extreme conditions of poverty, war, violence, and more, who live each day dependent on God, who alone keeps and preserves them. Holding faithful in the midst of authoritarian states, with persecution and suffering constantly at hand, the church faces enormous pressures to surrender its identity, to compromise in the face of such trials, and to neglect or distort its mission. The ever-present danger of the church being hypocritical towards God, towards itself, and towards the world is unavoidable. The church's inclination to teach and preach a gospel it fails to practice, especially in relationship to the poor and the marginalized, adds still more to the list of dangers and challenges faced by the church.

In this global season, it is not difficult to understand why the church is in pain and declining in its Christian and moral influence. No one is surprised in today's world about the fact that many so-called Gen Z's and Millennial's, for example, have no time for the church or Christianity. We can find this pattern around the world, but especially in urban centers. The reasons are many, but "church" and "Christianity" are assumed to be irrelevant, problematic, or probably worse. Furthermore, this is not just a pattern for youth and younger adults, but people in their middle and older years too. For devout people of

Christian faith, such condemning conclusions can seem simplistic and unfair; but for oceans of younger and multi-aged adults, these disaffected opinions are justified and self-evident conclusions. We might even say they are convictions reached by doing what seems to come naturally in this era and in places across the globe.

Every pastor and church leader who may be reading this knows many faces in this sea of disregard and disaffection. Hopefully, we are highly attentive in our roles, listening as carefully and deeply as we can to what this phenomenon is telling us. If we are tending flocks that are dissipating, we need to ask why it is happening, and how we pursue the sheep that are not just lost by circumstances, but by deliberate choice.

ReThinking Church in the 21st Century is an effort begun in 2021 to gather Christian leaders from a diverse range of backgrounds and nationalities online in order to listen to what gratitude and concerns we had about the state of the church as seen from many different angles. We were all Protestants, broadly evangelical, deeply committed to the holistic gospel of Jesus Christ, in varying roles of theological, pastoral, organizational, and congregational responsibility. We came together for an initial six months, and our work has gone on for an additional two and a half years. These three books are the product of the international members (and others) of the group, and the USA leaders have produced a multi-episode podcast. All of us have tried, within the bounds of our many other responsibilities, to contribute to our common cause. The community God has built among us during these years through hours and hours of online video conversations, and through our writing collaboration has been a gift beyond what we could initially have imagined, forming and strengthening enduring friendship in Christ.

The three volumes in this series are responses to the top three priority concerns that we determined are needed: *Suffering and Persecution*, led by Dr. Myrto Theocharous of Greece, *Metaphors the Church Lives By*, led by Dr. Elizabeth Sendek of Colombia, and *Faith and Public Life*, led by Dr. Alfred Sebahene of Tanzania. General Editors are Dr. Riad Kassis and Dr. Mark Labberton. We are very grateful for the contributions of all of our writers in each volume, here briefly summarized by our Volume Editors:

In *Suffering and Persecution* a variety of scholars and church leaders from or in the Majority World interact with writings, mostly from non-Western contexts, on topics such as violence, natural disasters, and ancient and modern persecution, and present their own reflections on these writings. The hope is that this volume will make available a variety of perspectives on suffering and persecution, and invite personal or communal contemplation on these universal themes. —**Myrto Theocharous**

We explore in *Metaphors the Church Lives By* seven biblical metaphors that are foundational for our understanding of the church in the twenty-first century. They transcend historical and sociopolitical categories. Three come from the gospels: *yeast, salt, light*; another three come from the Pauline epistles: *temple, body and ambassadors*; and one comes from the Petrine letters: *people of God*. The aim is to engage readers with the conceptual content of the metaphors and how they intend to shape experience and attitudes, so that we can live them out today. —**Elizabeth Sendek**

Times have changed. The global public space is filled with myriads of challenges. We live in an era which allows new contradictions and opportunities to emerge. But the love of God and the gospel of Christ never changes. How then should the church be engaged in the public space of the twenty-first century? *Faith and Public Life* seeks to answer this pertinent question by inviting Christians to respond with vigor to Christ's call to follow him in whole-life discipleship in this century and beyond. Throughout the pages of this book, Christians from diverse walks of life have given Bible-based testimonies about life in the public square, one of the arenas in which believers' love of God and love of neighbors must be exhibited. The book calls the church and Christian believers to constantly review how to proclaim and serve in the world while appreciating evident signs and wonders witnessing to the nature and character of God, especially his grace. —**Alfred Sebahene**

In these volumes each author speaks for themselves only, and not as a representative of any organization or institution. We offer our great thanks for individuals whose generous financial contributions made this effort possible. They are people with hearts full of the grace of God and love for the church.

Our hope is that these books will prompt pastors and thoughtful Christian leaders to be stimulated by these reflections and admonitions during such a dynamic, vulnerable, and hopeful time as the twenty-first century is presenting. We believe that "God is the same yesterday, today, and forever," and that the church is alive in settings that are constantly changing. This is the intersection we take with great faith and seriousness as we trust the Lord Jesus Christ who reigns in love, justice, and mercy.

To God's glory and honor, and for the welfare of God's church around the globe, we dedicate these books.

Riad Kassis and Mark Labberton

General Editors:	Riad Kassis (Lebanon), Mark Labberton (USA)
Series Editor:	Joshua Barron (Kenya)
Volume Editors:	Alfred Sebahene (Tanzania)
	Myrto Theocharous (Greece)
	Elizabeth Sendek (Colombia)
Meditations Editor:	Milton Acosta (Colombia)
Dialogue Participants:	Wojciech Szczerba (Poland), Antonio Carlos Barro (Brazil), David Tarus (Kenya), Jonathan Kavusa (Democratic Republic of Congo), Sergiy Tymchenko (Ukraine), Alejandra Ortiz (Mexico), Antonina Szczerba (illustrator; Poland)
Illustrations:	Antonina Szczerba (Poland)
Administration:	Stefanii Morton, Mandy Macintosh

Volume Introduction

The invitation was enticing and sobering:

> You are invited to be part of a new initiative called: ReThinking
> Church for the 21st Century. I believe it comes to you out of an
> urgent sense of timeliness, challenge, and opportunity.
>
> This deliberate, but informal, effort is meant as an act of love
> for Christ, crucified and risen; an act of love for the Body of Christ,
> blessed and broken; an act of love for God's world, violent and lost.
>
> You are invited to join the Working Group of approximately
> 15 highly diverse international men and women, for Phase 2 of
> this project. We spent the second half of 2021 in listening, prayer,
> burden-bearing, story-telling, study, reflection, imagination, and
> discernment – all focused on reconsidering the life of the Church
> at a time when Christ's Bride seems exceptionally divided, tur-
> bulent, guilty, and vulnerable. We now want to work together to
> create some resources to invite others into this conversation.

Accepting it has meant a commitment of two and a half years to delve into
the theology and identity of the church in the twenty-first century around the
globe. The process of reflection and discernment resulted in the definition of
the book we have written to serve the church of today and of tomorrow in
this century.

Our group of five was geographically diverse (Brazil, Colombia, the United
States, Poland, and Ukraine), but we shared a common history of involvement
in theological education, so a key question was raised: How could we speak
about the identity and theology of the church in a way that resonates beyond
our generation and our pursuits as theological educators? The New Testament's repeated use of metaphors to speak of the church guided us to center
our work in some of them. To further our understanding of what metaphors
are and how they function we read the seminal work of George Lakoff and
Mark Johnson, *Metaphors We Live By*[1] and invited a young pastor and scholar,
Dr. Oscar Jiménez, to share with our group about the contributions of cognitive linguistics to biblical studies. He helped us see metaphors as "conceptual

---

1. Chicago: University of Chicago Press, 2003.

mapping[s] that can shape or alter the perception as well as define or solidify identity of the member of a discourse community."[2] We are very grateful for his contribution. The addendum to this introduction, "The Metaphorical Character of Language," expands on this.

This is a book written for pastors and lay leaders who, as followers of Jesus, seek to be his credible witnesses, while acknowledging the current deep crisis we face as the church. We write for an audience of real people who strive to walk in coherence with their faith and who aspire to engage younger generations to live the reality of the gospel. Challenging that walk are issues which profoundly affect the church, such as: identity defined more in sociopolitical terms than by the centrality of the cross and the resurrection, deficiencies in the formation of disciples, power abuses, diverse types of divisions, inadequate theological formation, declining credibility among young people and in the public square, technological disruptions and possibilities, etc.

The book expounds seven biblical metaphors that are foundational for our understanding of the church in our century. They transcend historical and sociopolitical categories. Their emphasis is not on human effort yet address real issues of living as the church today. It is not a book about the shortcomings of the church, but one that nurtures hope grounded in remembering who she is and that calls us to live that identity into the twenty-first century. Three come from the gospels: *yeast, salt, light.* Another three come from the Pauline epistles: *people, temple, body and ambassadors.* One comes from the Petrine letters: *people of God.* The aim is to engage readers with the conceptual content of the metaphors and how they intend to shape experience and attitudes, so we can flesh them out in our days and contexts.

Chapter one focuses on two risks posed by the metaphor of salt (Matt 5:13): losing the saltiness that should mark as us followers of Jesus and emphasizing function over essence in our understanding of the nature and purpose of the church. Chapter two addresses the metaphor of ambassadors of Christ (2 Cor 5:20) and the concomitant duty of representing Christ and his message in this world. It traces the sequence from Jesus as ambassador of God, disciples as ambassadors of Jesus, and the church as ambassador of God. Chapter three explores the relationship intended by God with his people and how he uses sacred spaces to manifest his presence among them. It offers a survey of the tabernacle and the temple in the Old Testament, followed by the New Testament declarations of Jesus as the one greater than the Temple and believers being the

---

2. Oscar Jiménez, unpublished notes presented to the Theology and Identity group on 15 August 2022.

Temple, with its implications for Christian living. Chapter four expounds how the metaphor of yeast (Luke 13:20–21) "points the Church towards the power of its authentic identity, and away from the power that is too often its delusion."

Chapter five focuses on how the "people of God" metaphor used by Peter (1 Pet 2:9–10) addresses matters of identity and belonging for Christians living as migrants. It concludes: "we can embrace our identity as the people of God, acknowledging that our allegiance is ultimately to Christ and his agenda . . . As God's people, we have a narrative for life."

Chapter six explores two requirements for the church underscored by the metaphor of light (Matt 5:14–16): to be distinct from the world and to be connected to Jesus. Chapter seven completes the work as it surveys the use of the body metaphor through history and in the Pauline epistles. It underscores the richness it brings to our understanding of the church in terms of belonging and solidarity, while acknowledging some negative connotations of its use by the church.

Gratitude is owed to Oscar Jiménez and John Jusu, who accepted the invitation of the group to contribute chapters to this book. They added to the geographical and experience diversity of the original group. We are particularly grateful for the gifted Antonina Szczerba, who enriched each chapter with her drawings.

We offer this work as an act of love for Christ, an act of love for His people, an act of love for His world. We pray that pondering on these seven metaphors helps Christians in different contexts "remember and embody our identity in the communion of the Father, Son and Spirit, and thereby in communion with those who seek to live the Jesus Way."[3]

Elizabeth Sendek
July 2024

---

3. ReThinking Church in the 21st Century Phase One (May 2021 – December 2021): Mapping the Issues. Unpublished document.

Addendum to Introduction

The Metaphorical Character of Language

Modern linguists convince us that language is conventional in its nature. We simply agree in various cultural-linguistic groups or families that we name things, states, actions, or ideas in certain ways using certain signs built of certain phonemes. We also agree in a conventional way as to the rules of how we create and combine linguistic signs in phonology, morphology, or syntax. Languages do not only describe reality or symbolize our thoughts; they also function as codes in the process of communication between senders and recipients.[1] There are various bases for the rules, which form languages, but most of the time they are very pragmatic in their nature. Languages are simply used and they practically evolve in time in the process of being used.

So, the declination of nouns or pronouns in the English language may be simpler now than it used to be a hundred years ago; in the Polish language, double negation is commonly used even though it is against the basic rules of logic and was unthinkable even in the eighteenth or nineteenth century; and German language is written today in a different, easier way than at the turn of the nineteenth and twentieth centuries. Not many people these days are able to easily decipher the old way of writing. So, languages – historically speaking – are created, shaped, and modified by people as they communicate. At the same time, people inherit languages, and adopt the codes of communication, as they learn them in various social contexts, usually in families or/and in schools. In this way languages serve not only as tools of communication; they are also tools of imagination; they shape people's thinking and their perception of reality. We may say that languages make people think of reality in a certain way.

The conventional character of language indicates that there is no direct translation of reality as it appears to us into linguistic codes. Languages are

---

1. John. R. Taylor, *Cognitive Grammar*, Oxford Textbooks in Linguistics (Oxford: Oxford University Press, 2003), 36.

xvi   Metaphors the Church Lives By

simply conventions accepted, used, and developed by people and lately by machines in the process of communication. They refer to reality in a similar way as maps refer to certain geographical areas. Maps are not terrains; they are symbolic records of three-dimensional regions. Yet, they help us to move from one place to another, they also enable us to imagine what the geographic area looks like. Maps function well as guidelines for the symbolized territories, still, they are not territories. In a similar way languages, as some kind of codes, enable communication and description of various aspects of reality.

In these processes, various devices are used in languages, and metaphors are of fundamental importance.[2] Metaphor can be understood as "a figure of speech in which a word or phrase literally denoting one kind of object or idea is used in place of another to suggest a likeness or analogy between them, as in "A mighty fortress is our God.""[3] Cognitive linguists like Janet Soskice,[4] George Lakoff, and Mark Johnson have demonstrated that metaphors are not only used in poetry or broadly understood literature as some kind of rhetorical ornaments, but they are natural and very common means of expression in everyday language. Phrases like *black sheep, early bird, heart of gold, better half, night owl, melting pot*, and a multitude of others are constantly used to describe and denote something else than their literal reference. Metaphorical phrases use common, everyday references and physical experiences to express more abstract ideas or new concepts. They may be understood, imagined, or evoked through connotations with our well-known experiences. Love can be easily expressed as a common journey, time as money, something very valuable, and discussion as a conflict or even fight. With reference to new technologies, we talk of palmtops, computer mice, or satellite dishes. Yet, cognitive linguists tell us that metaphors are not only ways of expression of complex, esoteric, difficult, or new ideas in terms of something well-known to us and well-experienced by us, but actually metaphors most of all reflect our way of thinking. They are not only matters of language in terms of expressing something, they are

---

2. George Lakoff and Mark Johnson, *Metaphors We Live By*, 2nd edition (Chicago: University of Chicago Press, 2003). Also see Barbara Dancygier and Eve Sweetser *Figurative Language, Cambridge Textbooks in Linguistics* (Cambridge: Cambridge University Press, 2014); Zoltán Kövecses, *Metaphor: A Practical Introduction*, 2nd edition (Oxford: Oxford University Press, 2010); Raymond W. Gibbs Jr., *Metaphor Wars: Conceptual Metaphors in Human Life* (Cambridge: Cambridge University Press, 2017); Jeanette Littlemore, *Metaphors in the Mind: Sources of Variation in Embodied Metaphor* (Cambridge: Cambridge University Press, 2019); Janet Martin Soskice, *Metaphor and Religious Language* (Oxford: Clarendon Press, 1985).

3. *Merriam-Webster.com Dictionary*, s.v. "metaphor," https://www.merriam-webster.com/dictionary/metaphor

4. Janet Martin Soskice, *Metaphor and Religious Language* (Oxford: Clarendon Press, 1985).

mainly matters of understanding the world and only then of translating the metaphorical comprehension of reality into language-code of communication, which subsequently leads to certain actions and/or attitudes.

In our thinking – as we are born in certain cultures and within them in certain languages – there are inscribed cognitive metaphorical structures, which help us to grasp the complex reality around and inside of us, and then to express it in a way that is comprehensible to others. So, even though languages are conventional and as such created in the development of humanity; even though the languages evolve as they are used, we – as individuals – not so much produce languages, but rather inherit them, and with languages we inherit metaphors. The physical, basic connotations, on which metaphors are based then not only refer to our own experiences, but quite often they reflect the experiences of the culture, the society in which we are born, and also the experiences of humanity as such. Metaphorical patterns are not so much our private property but rather shared cultural and linguistic models of experience. Birth, death, love, hate, fight, food, water, eating, sleeping, plants, animals, stars, planets, sky, day, night, home, work, and so on, are just a few examples of realities and experiences that all people share. On them are based our conceptual metaphors, understood as pervasive imaginative structures in human understanding of reality.

Wojciech Szczerba

1

The Salt of the Earth

Elizabeth Sendek

You are the salt of the earth. But if the salt loses its saltiness, how can it be made salty again? It is no longer good for anything, except to be thrown out and trampled by men. (Matt 5:13, NIV[1])

Introduction

Salt is a common substance used in everyday life in every culture. Throughout history, it has played a crucial role in food preservation. The expression "you are the salt of the earth" has become popular even beyond religious contexts. In some cultures, it is used colloquially to refer to decent and humble people; in others, someone with salt is likeable and charming. It is also the title of several books, poems, and songs. In religious settings, scholars and preachers explain what Jesus meant when using the metaphor to explain what it means to his followers today. They often point out the use of salt as a condiment, preservative, and additive to manure.

Such familiarity with salt and the image of people as the salt of the earth has been appropriated in different cultures and settings, making it fundamental to ground our understanding of the seminal saying in the exploration of the text in the Gospel of Matthew.

> You are the salt of the earth. But if the salt loses its saltiness, how can it be made salty again? It is no longer good for anything, except to be thrown out and trampled by men (Matt 5:13)

---

1. All Scripture quotations in this chapter are taken from the NIV.

Jesus designates his followers metaphorically with a simple, common, and unsophisticated element: salt. Although salt was very valuable in the ancient world, it was neither unknown nor unfamiliar to people. Upon hearing this comparison, Jesus's audience would have thought of their own direct or indirect experience with salt, used their imagination to connect that experience to what Jesus might have intended in the flow of the discourse where the metaphor was expressed, and continued pondering about it to grasp the meaning of his simple words.

In first-century Palestine, Jesus and his disciples would have been aware of the domestic use of salt in flavouring and preserving food, and of its agricultural usage as an additive to manure employed as fertilizer (Luke 14:34–35). Salt was also indispensable for the sacrificial practices of the Jerusalem temple. It was necessary to season the daily offerings that were central to its liturgy. The use of salt in offerings represented God's covenant loyalty to Israel (Lev 2:13) and with those he chose for his service (Num 18:19; 2 Chr 13:5). In brief, salt implied a commitment to covenant agreement. It was also used to preserve the hides of sacrificed animals, which became the property of the priests. The Dead Sea was recognized as the primary source of salt for people in Palestine. A steady supply was secured from this venue for temple use.[2] Of course, there were negative connotations of salt such as despair, death, desolation, and unproductive land. But they are not the focus of Jesus's saying.

Centuries later, the metaphor still causes us to think of our conscious and unconscious encounters with salt in daily life. Our most common referent is table salt: refined, present in kitchens worldwide, enhanced with spices, and even hailed from exotic places. However, it has other uses in manufacturing processes and products that regularly touch our lives: leather, soap and detergents, processed foods, pharmaceutical products, cattle feed, rubber, pottery, and glass. It is also used in the unclogging of plumbing, de-icing of roads, and fixating of colours in cloth. Salt is ever-present, so familiar, and often unnoticed. When we read or hear Jesus's saying, like the disciples, we must ponder what he means.

One approach to the metaphor is through the lens of household food preservation and flavouring. Different elements enter in play: food items (what needs to be preserved and flavoured – vegetables, meats, etc.), containers in which food is preserved, salt as the fundamental preservative and flavouring

---

2. Reid. Daniel G. "Sacrifice and Temple Service." In *Dictionary of New Testament Background*, edited by Craig A. Evans and Stanley Porter, 1036–1050, esp. 1044. Downers Grove: InterVarsity Press, 2000.

element, and the salting process and its result. At the positive end, core concepts include freshness, wholesomeness, and the quality of food being maintained through effective preservation practices. Yet there is also a threat in the
form of spoilage and corruption – the very reason why salt is mainly used.
Most language used cross-culturally to talk about salt stems from understanding it through this lens. At the centre of it stands salt itself, the critical element
that enhances flavour and/or maintains wholesomeness from spoiling.

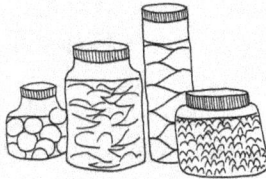

Through this lens, when Jesus metaphorically calls his disciples "the salt of
the earth," they correspond directly to the salt – infused within the "container"
of the world to influence the realm around them. Earth represents the domain
that salt is to permeate, corresponding to the vessels that store preserved foods.
Just as salt uniquely maintains edibility and flavour, Jesus's disciples have the
special function of retaining and radiating the core ethical virtues that inhibit
moral decay in society. These processes enhance and spread desirability, while
avoiding corruption. Thus, Jesus's followers become essential to human societies by preserving righteousness amid spiritual spoilage. As the expressions
cited at the beginning of this chapter communicate, societies even outside
religious contexts have deeply appreciated the qualities of humility, reliability,
and moral character, recognizing salt's universal value as a preserver.

Many contemporary interpretations of the metaphor reflect this framework, concentrating on the function of salt and what it implies. The following
question which introduces an unexpected twist in the metaphor is addressed
less frequently: If salt loses its saltiness, can it still be considered salt? Not that
Jesus is not interested in the usefulness of salt; however, his disturbing concern
is salt losing its essence.

Jesus and his listeners knew that salt could in fact lose its flavour because
it was not pure; it was mixed with other chemicals present in the water of the

Dead Sea.[3] Crystalized salt could also absorb humidity, which would dissolve and rinse away the sodium chloride. When the humidity evaporated, the resulting product looked like salt but was no longer salt. Even worse, it did not taste like salt nor did it perform the functions of salt.[4] Hence, the disciples got the point of the metaphor, and that point stuck in their minds – both Mark and Luke include it in their gospels (Mark 9:49–50; Luke 14:34–35).

This twist from function to essence invites another approach: reading the metaphor through the lens of ontological essence, where the emphasis lies specifically on saltiness itself – the innate purity and integrity that defines true salt. This focus on salt's ontological essence signals that Jesus focuses more on being rather than doing. When Jesus posed the risk of salt losing its saltiness, he targeted corrupted essence, not compromised effectiveness. Salt's subsequent worthlessness stemmed not from failing functions but from defiled identity. To be "salt" requires carrying intrinsic traits of genuineness. In this light, Jesus's teaching highlights disciples embodying a personification of saltiness – wearing their fundamental virtues as an identity rather than wielding their variable uses as a set of tools. The loss of saltiness represents nullified skills due to the devastated corruption of moral character.

Jesus raises several questions beyond the function of salt. Several of these questions are answered when the metaphor is considered in the context of the Sermon of the Mount: who is being addressed? How has the audience been previously described? What is the essence that should be preserved in order to be useful as salt and not scorned? What is implied in setting the earth as the sphere of functioning as salt? What does the metaphor mean today?

3. Harrington, Daniel J. *The Gospel of Matthew*. Sacra Pagina 1. Collegeville: Liturgical Press, 1991, esp. 80.

4. France, R. T. *The Gospel of Matthew*. New International Commentary on the New Testament. Grand Rapids: Eerdmans, 2007, esp. 174–175. See also Millos, Samuel Pérez. *Mateo. Comentario exegético al texto Grieto del Nuevo Testamento*. Barcelona: Clie, 2009, esp. 306–307.

The Metaphor in Context: the Beatitudes and Saltiness

Matthew 5:1–2 establishes Jesus as a teacher who instructs his disciples as his primary audience in the presence of a multitude. His discourse opens with a series of bold claims that have become known as the Beatitudes. These descriptions are Jesus's call to his followers to "be" in ways that lead to real thriving. This idea comes from the Old Testament, where each beatitude describes persons who flourish in the context of their covenant relation with God.[5]

The way of being set out in Jesus's assertions is what makes his disciples distinctive from those around them, because their flourishing, although marked by suffering, is rooted in the hope that God will eventually make everything right when the kingdom proclaimed and inaugurated by Jesus (Matt 4:17) comes in its fullness. The beatitudes are not a disconnected classification of types of people, nor an emotional state of wellbeing, neither are they a personal improvement plan to attain the goal of happiness. They constitute a whole that describes the qualities that should ideally characterize each member of the community of his followers. What he states as virtues are paradoxical proposals that subvert conventional wisdom about what produces fulfilment and plenitude. The first half of each beatitude focuses on a characteristic that signals adversity; they seem to be conditions to avoid if one is to succeed in life. The second half of each beatitude explains why that initial assertion, despite initial appearances, is true and makes sense: its fruition rests on the blessings of the kingdom of God. To understand what it meant by being the salt of the earth it is necessary to explore this way of life. Matthew 5:3–12 is a good place to start.

5. Pennington, Jonathan T. *The Sermon on the Mount and Human Flourishing: A Theological Commentary.* Grand Rapids: Baker Academic, 2017, esp. 44–45, 50.

[3] Blessed are the poor in spirit,
  for theirs is the kingdom of heaven.
[4] Blessed are those who mourn,
  for they will be comforted.
[5] Blessed are the meek,
  for they will inherit the earth.
[6] Blessed are those who hunger and thirst for righteousness,
  for they will be filled.
[7] Blessed are the merciful,
  for they will be shown mercy.
[8] Blessed are the pure in heart,
  for they will see God.
[9] Blessed are the peacemakers,
  for they will be called children of God.
[10] Blessed are those who are persecuted because of righteousness,
  for theirs is the kingdom of heaven.

[11] Blessed are you when people insult you, persecute you and falsely say all kinds of evil against you because of me. [12] Rejoice and be glad, because great is your reward in heaven, for in the same way they persecuted the prophets who were before you.

The poor in spirit live in total dependence on God, not only spiritually, but in every realm of life. They flourish because they are nurtured by the resources of God's kingdom without being disgraced, as would have been the case in the honour and shame culture of Jesus and his disciples. Those who mourn may weep in repentance, as frequently stated. It is also probable that Jesus is considering those who are hurt by the wickedness, death, and injustice of others. Matthew has already set the prophecy of Isaiah as a referent for the mission of Jesus (4:12–17). As the Messiah, his mission includes healing those whose hearts have been broken by different evils (Isa 61:1–2). The weepers flourish because they are promised God's consolation.

Those who choose to be humble and gentle in their interactions with others, even those who hurt them, rather than responding in kind by being harsh, aggressive, or cruel, are destined to inherit the earth.[6] Their internal fortitude and flourishing rest in God's unfailing promise: the meek will inherit the land and enjoy great peace (Ps 37:11). People who refuse to accommodate

---

6. Louw, Johannes, and Eugene Nida. *Greek-English Lexicon of the New Testament Based on Semantic Domains*, vol. 1. New York: United Bible Society, 1989, 749.

to the injustices around them and instead possess a compelling longing for justice, akin to the essential human needs of bread and water, will also thrive. They seek God's intervention and strive for moral and social rectitude, rather than remaining indifferent or complicit. They flourish because God himself will fill their hungry and thirsty hearts. The following chapters of Matthew's gospel showcase God's higher justice.

The mercy shown to those who are struggling, as well as their prosperity, stems from God's mercy bestowed upon them. In the reference to the pure in heart, the disciples may have heard echoes of Psalm 24:3–6. Access to God's presence is granted to those whose pure hearts make them authentic when dealing with God and others. In humility, they acknowledge that their vindication is not their own but comes from God. It is in fellowship with him that they flourish. A common Latin-American saying states that a tiger's cub is born with stripes, meaning children reflect the traits of their parents. Peacemakers flourish because, in seeking peace, they are recognized as God's children. They take after their Father who, in Jesus, seeks his enemies in order to reconcile them with him.

The last beatitude stands in tension with the previous one: peacemakers may not always attain peace, instead they may suffer persecution for their firm commitment to righteousness. Though they are rejected in the world, the kingdom of God is theirs so they continue to flourish. Expanding on the theme of persecution, Jesus addresses his disciples directly for the first time: "blessed are you . . ." Jesus's disciples find themselves in good company when they face persecution, as they are joined by those during the Old Testament era who endured mistreatment and remained steadfast in their faith. They can rejoice because God's reward is secured in heaven. They can stand their persecution with joy because, although they may lose everything on earth, they have everything in heaven.

The state of blessedness or flourishing that Jesus invites his disciples to experience rests on the promises of future fulfilment. However, the first and last beatitudes are exceptions: the poor in spirit and the persecuted already partake of a reality that is yet to be fully fulfilled; they have already entered God's kingdom.[7]

The beatitudes present descriptors rather than functional imperatives. Adjectives like "poor," "meek," "merciful," denote qualitative attributes, not

---

7. Sandez, Sydney de Moraes. "Mateo." In *Comentario Bíblico Contemporáneo*, edited by René Padilla, Milton Acosta, and Rosalee Velloso, 1163–1217, esp. 1173. Buenos Aires: Certeza Unida, 2019.

action verbs (though actions must follow). They stress who the disciples fundamentally ARE, much more than what they DO. Just as "salty" signifies an essential quality of purity, the beatitudes signify states to personify. The beatitudes' adjective-centric emphasis highlights the priority this metaphor places on the sanctity of what a disciple IS at one's ontological root before righteousness propagates through action. Together, they depict the core virtues that characterize Jesus's true followers. Those who exhibit this way of being and living are the ones Jesus calls the salt of the earth. Setting the earth as the domain of their usefulness stands in tension with the honorary risk of insult, persecution, and slander just discussed.

As previously mentioned, the focus is not on food preservation but on the ontological essence of salt. The risk Jesus points out is clear: should salt lose its saltiness, its essence, it would become useless. To contemporary ears, the notion that salt may become saltless is absurd because we are used to refined table salt, which may clump, but not lose its flavour, except when it is overdiluted. As we have noted, salt in the times of Jesus was not the purified, refined condiment we are familiar with. It *was* possible that salt could lose both its taste and its usefulness. The impossibility of salt regaining its taste serves as a sobering reminder of what would happen next: it would be crushed under the feet of people. To Jesus's immediate hearers the idea that living the Beatitudes may entail suffering but ultimately lead to vindication by God even though one has lost one's essence and usefulness would bring scorn – for the metaphor stressed the likelihood of ruination and highlighted the importance of preserving one's saltiness.

The Metaphor Today

What does the metaphor reveal about the nature of the people of God in the twenty-first century? How does it affect our understanding of our identity and role as followers of Jesus Christ? To answer these questions, we need to examine our posture as his audience and determine where our primary focus should be when interpreting the metaphor.

Jesus's sermon, which includes the metaphor, was not addressed to the religious leaders of his time. In fact, this is true of all the discourses in this gospel. Therefore, the invitation to today's audience is to listen as disciples, not as religious leaders, protectors, or representatives of institutionalized religion. This implies a posture of humility, which is essential as we recognize that we live in times of deep disillusionment and a generalized lack of trust in authority figures and in religious institutions that have let people down.

In this chapter, I am not focusing primarily on the use of salt (a traditional approach). As mentioned, interpreters commonly offer a variety of meanings based on the use of salt in the Old and the New Testaments: flavouring, food preservation, purification, a symbol of covenant faithfulness, a sign of God's kingdom; some appeal to the popular idea that it means being likeable thus attracting people to Christ. Another common notion is that this function relates to the world beyond the church. After all, the usefulness of salt is only appreciated when it interacts with the elements it is supposed to affect, be it food, soil, wounds, etc.

Instead, the key concern Jesus communicates with the use of the metaphor is the preservation of the nature of salt so it can be useful. What does being salt entail? The radical ethical vocation of Jesus's followers is described in the beatitudes. These descriptions constitute the distinctive essence that makes Jesus's disciples the salt of the earth. To that vocation, their saltiness, they must remain faithful, because it is the foundation of their usefulness in the world. This implies that the fundamental concern of the church should be its essence and how this shapes its practice rather than focusing on activities and programmes, sometimes at the expense of the church's essence. In brief, activism does not necessarily mean usefulness for the gospel or God's mission.

The way of being the beatitudes invite us to embrace in the twenty-first century is just as opposite to what society promoted in Palestine in the first-century and what society is also promoting today. Society often disregards the virtues expected of the people of God and views them as signs of weakness and insignificance. Therefore, to follow Jesus implies a deconstruction of current human values, requiring a commitment to a way of being as radical and paradoxical as the kingdom of heaven itself, a kingdom whose fulfilment Jesus's disciples have eagerly anticipated throughout history. The character traits of the kingdom of God, often overlooked or despised in society, are considered praiseworthy. What counts is not the cunning or resourcefulness often valued in some cultures, for example, the Latin-American concept of *viveza* (cunning to obtain what is wanted without any effort or at the expense of others), but the strength that comes from a character that reflects God's righteousness. Therefore, the church is faced with two options that may equally lead to two contrasting outcomes: the condemnation of people for being useless or their contempt for adhering to principles that do not emphasize self-promoting and ruthlessness. Instead, they place their trust and hope in the blessings of God's kingdom, not in the good life attainable by human resourcefulness.

Pure salt, sodium chloride (NaCl), does not decompose by itself; it may become clumpy, but it is still salty. However, there are two ways in which it can effectively lose saltiness, both related to its interaction with other elements. It can become overdiluted when the salt concentration is too low in relation to the amount of liquid in which it is diluted, resulting in saltiness being watered down. It can also lose its flavour when it contains chemical impurities. This puts the community of disciples (the salt of the earth) in tension: its function is to serve beyond its confines, yet it is in interaction with society by which it can be watered down or contaminated. This same tension was expressed (differently) in Jesus's prayer for his disciples and their mission: they are sent to the world, but they no longer belong to the world. Hence, they are rejected. It is in that hostile environment that they are to remain faithful, trusting in God's protection (John 17:13–18). What does it look like for the church to lose saltiness today?

When claims of self-assurance, self-promotion, anointed authority, and exclusive ownership of the truth animate ecclesiastical discourse and practice, saltiness becomes diluted. Such pretences stand in opposition to a life of humble dependence on God. Jesus's disciples echo St. Teresa of Ávila's words: "God alone suffices."[8] A recent meme in social media reads: "The problem of our times is that Christians do not want to be useful, but to be important." Examples of this poignant truth are not hard to find in Latin America, where the evangelical church has grown from an insignificant minority in the first half of the last century to a group recognized as an important contributor to the transformation of the religious landscape in the region. With this numeri-

---

8. Teresa of Ávila (1515–1582) was a Spanish Christian mystic. The original Spanish is *solo Dios basta*. These words are an excerpt of a poem she had written on her bookmarks which was found after her death.

cal growth has also grown the craving for recognition as an important player in the political arena.

In pluralist societies, perspectives and agendas challenge the church on matters of gender, marriage, adoption, and abortion. In this milieu, saltiness is expressed in fortitude that comes from being dependent and vulnerable before God, thus refusing to turn into enemies of those who think and live differently. When neighbours become enemies, belligerence in speech and action is sanctioned, and discredit is fostered through labels that diminish their humanity and by a tangential relation with the truth. When the people of God consider gentleness to be weak, power becomes an idol. Meekness is not a lack of spine or conviction but the opposite of harshness, aggressiveness, or cruelty.

Salt does not adopt the flavours of the substances with which it interacts as its own. Similarly, the church should not be complicit with the lack of righteousness and justice in society. Although socially marginalized in many countries, members of evangelical churches were known to be trustworthy when evangelical churches were few in Latin America. As the church has grown numerically, the sad incidences of abuse, corruption, and injustice in its midst have also grown, resembling what happens in society at large. Where corruption is rampant, instead of remaining silent, the church should raise its voice against it and, at the same time, be a model of integrity and righteousness in all her ministerial and administrative activities. Such integrity would be conducive to the formation of upright disciples in all her relations and dealings, whether public or private. In this way, the church would be salt, not through religious discourse, but through evidence of probity. Hunger for justice is more than social activism; the longing for God's intervention must go hand-in-hand with purity of the heart. This refers to being a person whose public discourse is matched by what happens in private and being persons who do not erect themselves as a spiritual and moral elite standing in judgment over others. It means being the opposite of those who, although religious, reject the will of God, in fact being evildoers (Matt 7:21–22).

There are countless examples of the church taking care of the hungry, thirsty, marginalized, naked, migrant, sick, and prisoners, because that is the call of the gospel. In the majority of cases, sharing is not motivated by a sense of abundance, but rather by a spirit of generosity and a willingness to part with the few resources available, without the need for elaborate programmes or initiatives. During disaster situations in Latin America, it is customary for relief organizations to turn to churches as distribution agents for the goods they provide. This is because churches are often viewed as trustworthy institutions that can be relied upon to distribute aid without corruption. This is an example of saltiness, rather than benefiting from the weak and needy.

In recent decades, a long-standing and complex internal conflict has caused one of the darkest periods of violence in Colombia. A well-known sociologist was invited to speak at a national gathering of pastors. The main theme of his speech was that the church, with its understanding of forgiveness, was the key to bringing peace to Colombia. Forgiveness, he emphasized, is the only way to break the endless cycles of revenge and counter revenge that feeds war. Almost two decades later, most urban churches in the country voted against the peace agreement that could end the longest civil war in the Western hemisphere. Varied reasons were given for this; most of them revealed the same polarization of the country, rather than gospel-informed arguments. In this specific matter, the church's vote highlighted our genuine Colombian identity and how little of Christ we had. To this day, the victims in regions ravaged by violence have demonstrated a greater capacity to forgive and a deeper desire for reconciliation than most evangelicals. What failure in our calling to be peacemakers!

Peacemaking is not an appeasement nor does it necessarily diffuse attacks on the church. Peacemakers may end up being crucified, as was the case with Jesus, the Son of God, and the peacemaker par excellence. But not all the actions that the church perceives as attacks are motivated by antagonism toward the gospel.

In certain circumstances, what is perceived as persecution is actually the requirement for religious organizations to follow the same rules as all other sectors of society, such as the use of public spaces, fair taxation of commercial activities, and fair treatment of employees. In other instances and contexts, true persecution takes place, even to the cost of people's freedom and lives. Those who are persecuted not only stand in the company of those persecuted in the past, but also in the shadow of the slain and risen Lamb of the book of Revelation. This is the Lamb who shares his kingdom with these people (cf. Rev 2:26, 27; 3:21), not as compensation to victims, but because they have attained their ultimate triumph over adversity, even over the power of evil, by persevering in the path of the one they proclaim:

> They triumphed . . .
> by the blood of the Lamb
> and by the word of their testimony;
> they did not love their lives so much
> as to shrink from death. (Rev 12:11)

In an age when many feel threatened by pluralism and secularism, it is not uncommon (at least in Latin America) to see many Christians roaring like lions in the name of God Almighty, fighting for their rights or their favourite doctrines, seeking to persuade through coercion in order to feel safe. Yet our call is to live lives shaped by less self-preservation, more dependence; less self-sufficiency, more vulnerability; less belligerence, more integrity; less manipulation, more compassion; less complicit silence, and more faithfulness.

It is common to confuse what we do with the essence of our identity as the church. We maintain structures, rituals, and programmes that often reflect the milieu around us, more than the way of life that flourishes and seeks the flourishing of others. When that happens, we have lost our saltiness, we have betrayed our essence. When that happens, what we reap is the scorn of the society we seek to emulate and whose favour we court, the very society where the church becomes diluted, flavourless, worthless, and meaningless. It is a terrifying prospect!

Salt is just as effective in small or large quantities, depending on its intended use. Thus, the church – either in institutional ways or through the life of its members' private lives – is called upon to express the essence that makes it the salt of the earth. Evidence of faithfulness to the kingdom of God can be seen in numerous small yet deeply meaningful ways, even though these contributors often remain anonymous and go unnoticed.

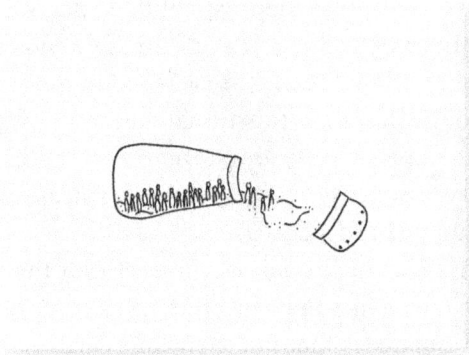

Some examples from the Colombian context are as follows: the only survivor of a massacre shares God's love and forgiveness with the attackers; the university professor who takes great personal and professional risks to stop corruption in the distribution of funds for research; church communities acting as effective agents of reinsertion of demobilized guerrilla members because it is a space where they can deal with their past, be embraced by a community, and look forward to a transformed life; temples turned into living quarters for persons in situations of displacement; the young urban pastor who, through his posts, encourages recognition of our failures as God's people in a tone that invites them to live out Christ's grace and transforming power.

Conclusion: Essence over Function

What does the metaphor reveal about the nature of the people of God in the twenty-first century? And how does it impact our perception of our identity and role as followers of Jesus Christ?

As the church we can persist in a verb-centric approach primarily focused on the functional uses and pragmatic impact of salt, orienting disciples toward tangible actions: salting the earth. Salt preserves food items, maintains freshness, infuses taste, and inhibits spoilage. According to this logic, the church's purpose revolves around activities and their efficiencies in "seasoning" the world and preventing increased moral decay. Therefore, a verb-first approach can become misguided and lead disciples to a utilitarian overprioritizing of flashy actions over Christlike essence. Judging effectiveness by visible impact rather than internal alignment with God may promote hypocrisy. But preserving Christlike "saltiness" must take precedence over rushing for visible change.

While important, this distracts from the deeper adjective-essence that is central to Jesus's teaching. An adjective-oriented approach stresses the intrinsic nature of disciples, not just their capabilities. Beginning with adjectival essence provides the root and framework for righteous action to blossom. When disciples' foundational beings are steeped in grace, humility, compassion, and hunger for justice, their functional saltiness flows freely into society. Just as salt's stable qualities enable long-term preservation despite invisibility, cherishing adjective-essence sustains gradual permeation of virtue however imperceptible. Being must fuel doing.

"The biblical images of the salt of the earth, of the light of the world, suggest something of the fact that the church has a representative function. Salt of the earth presupposes that not the whole earth is salt. The church has as church a function for the whole, in the whole, and is not simply a copy of something else. . . "[9]

9. Ratzinger, Joseph. *Salt of the Earth: The Church at the End of the Millenium. An Interview with Peter Seewald.* San Francisco: Ignatius Press, 1997, esp. 272.

2

The Church as Ambassador for Christ

Antonio Carlos Barro and Jorge Henrique Barro

Introduction

We are all familiar with the international roles of ambassadors and embassies. The ambassador represents the interests of a ruler or government of one country within a foreign domain. According to the Merriam-Webster Dictionary, an ambassador is "a diplomatic agent of the highest rank accredited to a foreign government or sovereign as the resident representative of their own government or sovereign or appointed for a special and often temporary diplomatic assignment." But what does it mean for the church to be Christ's ambassador in the world, or for individual believers to be his ambassadors? We know that the church is "the church of God" (Acts 20:28, ESV[1]) and, therefore, driven by the Spirit of God, who blows where and when he pleases (John 3:8). Who can say where, when, and how the church will go? For example, "the believers from among the circumcision" could never have imagined that one day in the future the gift of the Holy Spirit would be "poured out even on the Gentiles." For this reason, the evangelist Luke reports that these Jewish believers were "amazed" at the descent of the Spirit upon those uncircumcised, the gentiles, and "heard them speaking in other tongues and praising God" (Acts 10:45–46, NLT).

The church is more than a religious organization/organism. From a sociological perspective, the church is also a social community, formed by human beings who are citizens acting at all levels of society. This fact challenges us to have perspectives on how the church can take concrete actions for its rel-

---

1. All Scripture quotations in this chapter are taken from the ESV unless otherwise noted.

evance in this world and what this represents for the future. In a way, society presents challenges to the church, which, if not considered, can jeopardize its relevance and credibility. In the twenty-first century, church and society are both challenged by the globalization of the economy, modern technological trends, and the perennial problem of social inequalities. In our context, how should we serve as Christ's ambassadors?

More than two thousand years since the beginning of the Christian movement, we have sufficient resources to instruct the ecclesiastical community and its leaders that this exercise imperatively demands our attention in the present. If we fail to fulfil the mission in the current context, how can we dare to anticipate that the church will fulfil it in the future, for example, thirty years ahead? Our present is suitable for indicating the paths that the church must tread to be relevant tomorrow. This challenge resembles the responsibility assigned to the sons of Issachar, who were recognized as "men who had understanding of the times" (1 Chr 12:31).

Understanding temporal contexts will certainly provide us with insight into the paths and trends to be followed in the future. The question before us at this moment is how to play the role of an ambassador of Christ in a constantly changing world. Although it may seem like a simple question, at its core, it implies a profound discernment about crucial issues such as witness and evangelization, engagement with the world, interaction with diverse cultures, inter-religious relations, ethical responsibility, mediation and reconciliation, as well as challenges associated with technology and communication, among others.

The concept of being an "ambassador of Christ" emphasized by the Apostle Paul in 2 Corinthians 5:20, incorporates the profound responsibility of Christians to represent Christ and his message in this world. The analogy used by Paul, equating Christians to ambassadors acting on behalf of Christ, implies not only the transmission of the gospel but also the manifestation of divine love to others. This understanding has significant implications for the present and future of the church. Even amid adversities, Paul acknowledged his condition as an ambassador, as expressed in Ephesians 6, highlighting his dedication to tirelessly proclaim the "mystery of the gospel" (Eph 6:19). A thorough analysis of this perspective in the context of the Roman Empire during the time of Jesus allows us to grasp the concept and importance of more meaningfully being an ambassador of Christ.

Ambassadors in the Context of the Roman Empire in the Time of Jesus

The term "ambassador" finds its origin in the medieval Latin word *ambascia-tor*, which was in turn borrowed from a Gothic word. In the time of Jesus, the Latin noun *legatus* was used to express the idea of "ambassador" in the Western Roman Empire while in the Eastern Roman Empire the Greek verb πρεσβεύω (*presbeúō*) signified being, or being sent as, an ambassador. The government or emperor officially dispatched ambassadors to undertake diplomatic missions, intending to represent the power and authority of Rome in other lands or international negotiations. The necessity for an ambassador arose from the colossal scale of Roman colonization during its territorial expansion, establishing colonies in various parts of the known world. The Roman Empire expanded through the conquest of territories surrounding the Mediterranean, stretching across what are now Egypt to England, Morrocco to Turkey. Ambassadors represented Rome within local client kingdoms subservient to Rome and to polities outside of Roman control.

This explains the need, importance, and relevance of the Roman Empire in establishing its *legati* or *presbeúomen* and sending them to represent the empire's interests as ambassadors. An ambassador was educated and sent to perform the following functions.

- Official Representation: Ambassadors acted on behalf of Rome; they held the authority to negotiate, make decisions, and establish official agreements.
- Diplomatic Missions: Their responsibilities included establishing relations with other nations, concluding treaties, resolving disputes, and delivering crucial messages, that is, they played a crucial role in the Roman Empire's foreign policy.

- Authority and Respect: In foreign lands, they were treated with deference and respect; any disrespect was considered a significant affront to Rome and could have grave consequences.
- Diplomatic Immunity: They enjoyed legal immunity, being exempt from legal proceedings or punishments under local laws while on official missions, which ensured their safety and ability to perform their functions.
- Communication: They were responsible for conveying the messages and policies of the Roman government to other nations and vice versa, that is, they played a vital role in the exchange of information between the empire and other political entities.
- Hosting and Provision: It was the responsibility of host nations to provide accommodation and meet the needs of ambassadors – including housing, food, and security – during their stay.

This background and the context of the ambassadorial institution require special attention when considering the Apostle Paul's adoption of the term, ambassador, and his use of it as a metaphor for Christians being perceived and recognized as official representatives of Christ. Christians are entrusted by Christ to communicate his gospel and the message of reconciliation with God, dispatched to the world in accordance with the instruction: "Go into all the world and preach the gospel to the whole creation" (Mark 16:15).

Jesus as an Ambassador of God – He Who Sent Me

There is no explicit record of Jesus using the word "ambassador." However, this does not invalidate the applicability of this concept to his life and ministry. An ambassador is one who is sent. It is noteworthy that, on several occasions, Jesus used the expression "sent me," acknowledging that he came into the world as one sent by the Father to look after his interests. Jesus applied this "sent me" expression to himself on thirty-eight occasions in the gospels (once each in Matthew and Mark, three times in Luke, and thirty-three times in John).

As the numbers show, the prominence that the Apostle John gives to this expression in his narrative is impressive. Indeed, John wanted to draw attention to his readers by emphasizing the expression "sent me" (also "he who sent me" and "he [God] who sent me"). According to Francis DuBose, "The sending not only reflects the nature of God and reveals the purposes of God but also demonstrates the method of God."[2] Jesus, as God's ambassador, is his method.

Jesus declared total dependence upon and obedience to God, stating, "I can do nothing on my own . . . I seek not my own will but the will of him [God] who sent me" (John 5:30). Jesus's obedience is fully demonstrated in his words, affirming that "the works that the Father has given me to accomplish, the very works that I am doing, bear witness about me that the Father has sent me. And the Father who sent me has himself borne witness about me" (John 5:36–37). Jesus considers himself an ambassador of God, saying, "I have come in my Father's name" (John 5:43). Jesus is an ambassador not only for the Father but also in the name of the Father.

Disciples as Ambassadors of Jesus – In My Name

The expression "in my name" used by Jesus in the gospels indicates the idea of an ambassador – acting "in the name" of someone means acting with their authority, according to their character, and in alignment with their purpose. Besides being one who is sent, an ambassador represents the one who sent him. In this case, disciples are sent in the name of Jesus. Jesus told Ananias on the Damascus Road, concerning Paul: "Go, for he is a chosen instrument of mine to carry my name before the Gentiles and kings and the children of Israel" (Acts 9:15). The mission of the disciples, in the Great Commission of Matthew, is to "Go therefore and make disciples of all nations, baptizing them in the name of the Father and of the Son and of the Holy Spirit" (Matt 28:19). Conversely, some would claim to be ambassadors of Jesus but are not, and thus, lack his authority: "Many will come in my name, saying, 'I am he!' and they will lead many astray" (Mark 13:6).

In Mark's Great Commission, the idea of an ambassador also appears: "Go into all the world and proclaim the gospel to the whole creation . . . In my name, they will cast out demons; they will speak in new tongues; they will pick up serpents with their hands; and if they drink any deadly poison, it will not hurt them; they will lay their hands on the sick, and they will recover" (Mark 16:15, 17–18). The same can be observed in Luke's Great Commission: "repentance for the forgiveness of sins should be proclaimed in his name to all nations, beginning from Jerusalem. You are witnesses of these things" (Luke 24:47–48). The Apostle John includes the idea of an ambassador in his Great Commission

2. DuBose, Francis M. *God Who Sends: A Fresh Quest for Biblical Mission*. Nashville: Broadman, 1983, esp. 61.

when he states that, although not explicitly mentioning the expression in his name, it is fully implied in what Jesus said: "As the Father has sent me, even so I am sending you" (John 20:21). Jesus's ministry carries significant theological and practical implications for the concept of an ambassador. It is closely tied to the authority and power that Jesus conferred upon his followers to conduct his mission and represent him on earth.

- Authority and Delegation: When Jesus used the phrase "in my name," he granted his disciples the authority to act in his name. This authority was not based on their merits or abilities but on their connection with him as his followers. They were authorized to perform specific actions and tasks, such as healing the sick, casting out demons, and spreading the gospel, all in his name.
- Invocation of Jesus's Authority: Acting in the name of Jesus means invoking his authority and power. This implies the recognition that Jesus is the ultimate source of authority and that his name carries significant weight. Believers acknowledged Jesus as Lord and Messiah by doing things in his name. There are four important facets to this.
- Unity and Alignment: "In my name" also means being in alignment with the teachings, values, and character of Jesus. Those who act in his name are expected to represent him faithfully, following his instructions and teachings. This emphasizes the importance of unity among believers, all working together under the banner of Jesus.
- Prayer and Intercession: The phrase is also used in the context of prayer. In John 14:13–14, Jesus said, "whatever you ask in my name, this I will do, that the Father may be glorified in the Son. If you ask me anything in my name, I will do it." This means that when believers pray in the name of Jesus they are not just repeating a formula but approaching God with the understanding that their petitions are aligned with the will and purposes of Jesus.
- Responsibility and Accountability: The authority granted in the name of Jesus comes with responsibility. Believers are expected to use this authority wisely and for just purposes. This implies accountability to Jesus in how they exercise his name.
- Mission and Testimony: The use of the name of Jesus was a fundamental aspect of the disciples' mission to proclaim and spread the gospel. Acts 4:12 states, "And there is salvation in no one else, for there is no other name under heaven given among men by which we

must be saved." This underscores the exclusivity of salvation through Jesus and the importance of proclaiming his name.

The expression "in my name" applied to the ministry of Jesus signifies the authority, power, and responsibility granted to his followers to fulfil his mission on earth as his ambassador. This symbolizes alignment with his teachings and character, recognizing his supreme authority, and a call to represent him faithfully in all actions and endeavours.

The Church as Ambassador of God

The people of God, spread across Jesus's communities worldwide – "For where two or three are gathered in my name, there am I among them" (Matt 18:20) – represent Christ himself as his ambassadors. He is present through his Spirit in the lives of those gathered in his name. The church is not a community that lives for its own interests. More than being sent, the church is already sent as an ambassador to care for God's interests – this is what we call God's mission – as the representative of the kingdom of God, like a diplomatic agency assigned a special mission, with the primary focus on the comprehensive reconciliation between God and human and non-human creation.

What are some challenges for the church to faithfully fulfil its vocation as an ambassador of God today and in the future?

Seeking the Peace of Babylon – Our Exile

The current locus of the church, whether we like it or not, is not Judah! We are not yet in the New Jerusalem but in exile. We are the people sent by God to live in Babylon: "Build houses and live in them; plant gardens and eat their produce. Take wives and have sons and daughters; take wives for your sons, and give your daughters in marriage, that they may bear sons and daughters; multiply there, and do not decrease. But seek the welfare of the city where I have sent you into exile, and pray to the LORD on its behalf, for in its welfare you will find your welfare" (Jer 29:5–7).

The future of the church will depend on whether it will "seek the welfare of the city where I have sent you into exile" or, as it has often done, seek its own prosperity within its walls, thinking that the church is synonymous with the temple as the place for people to hide from the world. The place of the church is in exile! This is in complete alignment with Peter's urban missiology, which states: "Beloved, I urge you as sojourners and exiles to abstain from the passions of the flesh, which wage war against your soul. Keep your conduct among the Gentiles honourable, so that when they speak against you as evil-doers, they may see your good deeds and glorify God on the day of visitation" (1 Pet 2:11–12).

Many pastors and leaders read this text in the following way:

- Abstain from the world and not from the desires of the flesh
- Keep conduct within the church and not among the Gentiles
- Practice good deeds only for believers and not for the Gentiles.

We live in this era of polarization, witnessing much anger from churches and believers toward exile. Instead of seeking "the welfare of the city where I have sent you into exile" and praying "to the LORD on its behalf," we see a church more passionate about ideological wars than concerned with the genuine issues of exile. Through the prophet Jeremiah, God is clear in stating, "for in its welfare is your welfare."

The Context Affecting All Churches

The future of the church – in terms of its relevance or lack thereof – will depend on its commitment to causes in today's world. While these are many, the following come immediately to mind.

- Environmental Care: As climate change becomes an increasingly urgent global issue, the church must take responsibility for God's creation. This includes addressing environmental concerns and advocating for sustainable practices.
- Global Crises: The church faces the challenge of responding to global crises such as natural disasters, pandemics, famine, poverty, and

refugee situations, among many others. Providing humanitarian aid and support while maintaining its core mission is both inevitable and demanding.

- Moral and Ethical Issues: Contemporary society grapples with many moral and ethical dilemmas, such as human rights, social justice, gender, sexuality, and bioethics. The church must engage with these issues thoughtfully and compassionately, aligning its position with its core values and respecting diverse perspectives.
- Social Justice and Inequality: The church is called to address poverty, inequality, racism, and social injustice. These challenges require a commitment to advocacy, activism, and systemic change, promoting equality and justice within the church.
- Technology and Social Media: The digital age presents opportunities and challenges for the church. While technology enables global outreach and communication, it also raises issues related to online behaviour, misinformation, and the impact of social media on faith and community.

These contexts are just a few illustrations of what we find in the world today. The church, an ambassador of Christ, cannot be ignorant or alienated from this reality, which is not only a reality for today but increases with each step we take into the future.

Agents of Transformation in the World

When the Apostle Paul taught us about being ambassadors of Christ, he also added the task of promoting reconciliation. The term "reconciliation" suggests the world of finance. In simple terms, to reconcile is to zero out the debit with the credit. In biblical terms, our debt with God (Col 2:14) was torn apart with the sacrifice of Christ on the cross of Calvary. What we owed to God was precisely the sum of Christ's life. Any other payment would not zero out the debt.

When Paul states that we have this ministry, we see it in a dual sense. The first is to lead people to be reconciled with God. No matter the world in which a person lives, they need to return to their Creator. This return is only possible in Christ Jesus. The second dimension of this ministry occurs horizontally. As ambassadors in this world, it is the responsibility of every Christian to function as an agent of reconciliation, incorporating the task of peacemakers as Jesus teaches in the Sermon on the Mount (Matt 5:1–12). We live in a chaotic world of socioeconomic disparities that becomes more insoluble with each passing day. Wars that seemed unimaginable in the twenty-first century continue to decimate lives for a piece of land, tribal differences, or even unbridled vengeance.

It is in this world that God calls us to play our role as ambassadors. The dilemma is the Christians' limited awareness of their role in the world outside the temples. It is not a lack of capacity or ability on the part of Christians, as they perform all kinds of functions in society with high competence. The problem is that these functions are conducted without the basic foundations of the gospel. Jesus's instruction to be the salt of the earth and the light of the world cannot penetrate the consciousness of these believers. The salt does not season, and the light does not shine. Much of this lack of awareness is due to the Christians themselves who do not educate themselves biblically and theologically for God's mission. E. Stanley Jones warned us about this, stating, "One of the greatest mission fields, if not the greatest, is the church members who are bogged down in their trivialities, producing little or nothing, busy at being busy with little or nothing to show for it."[3]

These church members, even if dormant, were for Jones the group that should be made aware and revived for God's mission, that is, to be ambassadors of Christ in the world. In his words:

> In the church of the future, the most important test of its power of survival and of its survival with power will be its capacity to win the two-thirds of its membership who are caught in eddies of the inconsequential and the marginal, and are going round and round, getting nowhere and producing little or nothing – except motion. This group is the greatest mission field of the church. It must be changed from a field for evangelism into a force for evangelism.[4]

However, on the other side of this scene is the enormous deficiency of ecclesiastical leadership that continues to operate under the dichotomy between clergy and laity. Also, in the 1960s, J. C. Hoekendijk already pointed out that the future of the church would pass through a deep understanding of the pastor regarding his role in relation to the laity.[5] Certainly, this ideal is not something so simple and easy to be realized in our days due to the ecclesial model that takes shape in our contexts. In this fossilized model, the pulpit is

---

3. Jones, E. Stanley. *The Reconstruction of the Church – On What Pattern?* Nashville: Abingdon Press, 1970, 111–112.

4. Jones, *Reconstruction*, 113.

5. Hoekendijk, J. C. *The Church Inside Out*. Philadelphia: Westminster Press, 1966, see esp. 83–109.

the main stage of the church, and it is occupied by the pastor, the star of the community. In the mould suggested by Hoekendijk, the main stage of the church is set up in the world, and its main actors are the laity.

Being an ambassador for Christ in a world that becomes increasingly cynical and distant from the precepts of the gospel will be the great challenge for the church of the future and a huge task that needs to be faced by all who wish to see the seed of the kingdom of God spread among all nations. Laity, pastors, educators, theology professors, theological seminaries, missionary agencies, Christian magazines, etc. – all need to take on this important mission, sit around the table, set aside unnecessary religious differences, and focus on the task of making Christ known among all peoples.

Conclusion

The future church we desire must be built starting today. The other day in our biblical theology of mission class, we were reflecting with the students about the church of the future. This is a theme that fascinates us, and we are perplexed that the vast majority of our leaders do not spend even an hour talking to their leadership about what the church of the future will be like. We asked the students about what prevents us from having more meetings to discuss this. Some answers were quite interesting:

1. The church is not encouraged by leadership to exchange ideas about the future.

2. Pastors are complacent and content with the current state.

3. Pastors fear tampering with tradition and are accustomed to ecclesiastical routine.

4. The church of the future is not a spiritual matter to be addressed in churches.

Another interesting point was this: today's church is hindering the church of the future from fulfilling its mission. It is true! Only today's church can make tomorrow's church possible.

Therefore, in conclusion, we urge churches worldwide to initiate, within their respective contexts, a careful examination of what is happening in their region and formulate the questions: What will the church of the future look like in our region? What will the church of the future look like in our country? Our hope is that this process will lead the church to assume more positively and concretely its mission of being an ambassador for Christ in this world.

3

Temple, Church, and God's Presence

John Jusu

The LORD is in his holy Temple,
  Let all the earth keep silent before him.[1]

Enter into his gates with thanksgiving
  And into his courts with praise.[2]

One of the necessities in life is shelter – a place to live and call home. Many people save money to build a house or buy one. It is always unsettling to live in a rented house or to live in some other person's house where you are always a guest, especially if you are not part of that family. Your home is the place where you meet people and where people come to meet you. It is your physical address to the extent that your presence is associated with that house. People might meet you on the streets and talk to you but when they want to discuss profoundly serious issues with you, they would prefer to come to your house. The house symbolizes your presence.

In most parts of world, religion is associated with a place and space. In these places, adherents go to pray, worship, and give offerings to their various divinities. Adherents of traditional religions go to the shrine or sacred bush: Muslims go to the mosque while adherents of Eastern Religions go to temples. These sacred spaces provide an avenue for the religious practices of individu-

---

1. Habakkuk 2:20, NLT. Unless otherwise noted, all Scripture quotations in this chapter are from the NLT.

2. Psalm 100:4, KJV.

als and communities as they demonstrate the relationship between them and their various deities or representatives. In modern terms, we will say that each religion has a permanent address – be it in town, in the forest under a tree, or by a rock or a river. These places are considered "sacred" because they possess characteristics that transcend normal human activities, expectations, and realities.

Driving on the streets of African countries, especially those that are South of the Sahara, you will notice, if it is on a Sunday, people dressed in their flamboyant attires going to a specific place called "church" – another sacred place. For such people, the church is a physical place to go to meet God or where God meets them. I listened to two children talking about church. One said, "God comes to my church on Sunday morning." The other said "God comes to my church on Saturday morning, then He goes to your church on Sunday." People going to church to meet God or God coming to church to meet people demonstrates the most popular views about the church as a special, sacred place to meet God.

In this chapter, we will explore the relationship God desired to establish with his people and how he made his presence manifest amongst them. We will treat some of the ways God instructed his people to make provisions for him to live with them in the Old Testament and the New Testament. In this light, we shall pay specific attention to the temple and the church with a little said about the tabernacle.

God's Meeting Places in the Old Testament

God has always desired to be with his people. In Genesis 3, we notice that God would come to walk in the garden to have fellowship with Adam and Eve – until they sinned, and he drove them from this presence. From then on, God's

presence became symbolic. The idea of a symbolic place where God dwells can also be traced to the experience of Jacob (Gen 28:10–17). Jacob on his way to Haran had to rest at a certain place for the night. He slept and had a dream of a staircase reaching the top of the heavens. He encountered God in this place and when he woke up, he said, "What an awesome place this is! It is none other than the house of God, the gateway to heaven" (Gen 28:17) and in Genesis 28:19, he names the place *Bethel*, meaning *house of God*. For Jacob, the place where the ladder stood was the "gateway of heaven" the place where heaven meets the earth and where individuals can find access to God. Through this experience of Jacob, we learn that God can choose a place to identify with.

Often, after epiphanic encounters, the patriarchs would erect a commemorative altar. As the history of Israel progressed, these altars became associated with "sanctuaries" like the ones in Shechem (Gen 12:6–7), Beersheba (Gen 26:25), and Hebron (Gen 13:18).[3]

The Ark and Tabernacle

Throughout the book of Genesis and parts of Exodus, God appeared specifically to the patriarchs as individuals. However, the first time God's presence appeared to all of Israel was at the foot of Mount Sinai. These Sinai theophanies were different from the patriarchal theophanies in significant ways.[4] First, the Sinai appearances happened in one place – the "mountain of God." Moses did not associate the appearances with fixed shrines and the appearances happened in normal places in ordinary environments. Moses prepared the people for the Lord's appearance by consecrating them (Exod 19:14) and after three days the Lord descended on Mount Sinai in an enormously powerful way that terrified the people (Exod 19:18) to such an extent that they pleaded with Moses to talk to God and God to talk to him on their behalf (Exod 20:19). Since the people can no longer come to God, God would have to come to them.

After Moses delivered the Ten Commandments to Israel, God invited him and seventy-three elders to worship him at a distance but gave permission to Moses to climb up to the mountain with him. Moses stayed on the mountain for forty days and forty nights and during those moments, God commanded Moses, "Have the people of Israel build me a holy sanctuary so I can live among

3. For a discussion of such epiphanies see Lindblom, Johannes. "Theophanies in Holy Places in Hebrew Religion." *Hebrew Union College Annual* 32 (1961): 91–106.

4. Terrien, Samuel. *The Elusive Presence: The Heart of Biblical Theology*. San Francisco: Harper and Row, 1978, esp. 106–109.

them" (Exod 25:8). Since the children of Israel were at this time still moving, God further commanded Moses (Exod 26:1–37) to build the tabernacle, which was to be the mobile sanctuary of God's presence with his people. When Moses completed the work of building the tabernacle, "Then the cloud covered the Tabernacle, and the glory of the LORD filled the Tabernacle" (Exod 40:34). Just after the manifestation of God's presence (v. 38), God started to lead his people during the night by a pillar of fire and by a cloud during the day. God now dwells amongst his people and had a home amongst them in a tangible way. The symbolic presence of God amongst his people was significant because "in the absence of a representation of the Deity, the sense of divine nearness could hardly survive among the people at large. The idea of the omnipresence is too diffuse and vague for effective awareness of daily existence."[5] The tabernacle became the place where the Israelites made their offerings and sacrifices in worship of the Lord. Most Africans cherish the symbolic presence of deity. They use inanimate objects to represent the presence of God as in the Crucifix, rocks, rivers, and other wonders of nature. The physical church building in some Christian traditions is also called the tabernacle, especially among Africa Initiated Churches and some Independent Churches. Though the tabernacle was also called "the tent of meeting" (Exod 27:21), it was not a place where God's people came to meet collectively to worship God, but a place where God met with his people through representatives of the people.

The Temple

The visible presence of God remained in the tabernacle for more than 440 years until the time of King Solomon. During the reign of David, the Lord's pres-

---

5. Terrien, *The Elusive Presence*, 163.

ence was still domiciled in a tent, and this did not please David. He lamented the fact that he lived in a house made of cedar while God lived in a tent. He decided to build a permanent building for God and that place was to be the Israelite temple (2 Sam 7). Probably the idea of building a permanent resting place for the God of Israel was influenced by the neighbouring tribes who had built elaborate temples for their gods like the Philistine temple of Dagon in Ashdod (1 Sam 5:2–7), and the temple of Ashtoreth (1 Sam 31:8–10). However, God told Nathan to tell David that he (God) had never complained of living in a tent (2 Sam 7:7), and that David should not go ahead with his plan for several reasons.

The English word "temple" (Latin: *templum*) "originally signified an uncovered area marked off by boundaries; especially the place marked off by augurs [priests] to be excepted from profane uses."[6] It is noteworthy that the Hebrew word (*hekel*) which the English Bible versions have translated as "temple" did not always carry a notion of sacredness. It also meant a palace or a large luxurious house (1 Kgs 21:1). However, when *hekel* is paired with the name "Yahweh," as in "*hekel* Yahweh" (Yahweh's Palace or the LORD's Temple) as used in Jer 7:4; 24:1 and Ezek 8:16, the reference is specifically to the temple erected by Solomon in Jerusalem.[7] Thus, Haran concerning the temple indicates that "this name arises from the concept of the divine residence and expresses the intrinsic nature of the institution which was primarily conceived as the god's dwelling place."[8] God allowed King Solomon to build a temple – his palace – that was to be his dwelling place forever. However, Solomon realized that God cannot live on earth and hence could not live in the temple he had built. The physical space on earth ceases to be God's abode but became a place that bears the name of God. Consequently, in Solomon's prayer of dedication (1 Kgs 8:22–66), the physical temple became the means through which God's people could reach him and through which God could answer prayers and supplications from heaven. Solomon in his dedication called upon God to hear people when they pray in the temple, when they pray toward the temple, and when they take oaths in the temple, and God must hear them from heaven. When Solomon finished his prayers "fire flashed down from heaven and burned up the burnt offering and sacrifices, and the glorious presence of the Lord filled

---

6. Kleinschmidt, Beda, and Walter Drum. "Temple," in *The Catholic Encyclopedia*, vol. 14. New York: Robert Appleton Company, 1912, https://www.newadvent.org/cathen/14495a.htm.

7. Haran, Menahem. *Temples and Temple Service in Ancient Israel.* Winona Lake: Eisenbrauns, 1983, esp. 13–14.

8. Haran, *Temples and Temple Service*, 13.

the Temple" (2 Chr 7:1). In response to this prayer, God said to Solomon "I have heard your prayer and your petition. I have set this temple apart to be holy – this place you built is where my name will be honoured for ever. I will always watch over it, for it is dear to my heart" (1 Kgs 9:3). The physical building had become "the gateway to heaven."

Solomon's idea of the temple becoming a means of reaching God is repeated in some African traditional religions where inanimate objects and special things are used to reach to their gods. For example, the Mende of Sierra Leone would consider a tree, a mountain, or a river as special means of reaching their God. This is like Solomon's view that the temple is not the place where God lives, but a means of reaching God. Thus, these traditionalists believe that God can be reached through his creation.

The temple remained a sacred place in the life of the people of Israel also for 400 years during which time that first temple saw periods of abuse, attacks by Israel's neighbours, and times of reforms and restoration. The temple temporarily lost its significance when King Ahaz, to pay the temple tax to the King of Assyria, plundered the temple and built an altar in the temple that conformed to the worship of the Assyrians. Unfortunately, the temple that Solomon built was destroyed in 586 BC and the Israelites were deported to Babylon. The people of Israel lost the presence of God as the visible presence of God's covenant with his people was obliterated. God, as it were, had destroyed himself.

When Cyrus ascended the throne of Persia in 538 BC, he made provisions for the people of Israel to return to their homeland. When they returned, they immediately built an altar and began building the temple, which became the second temple. The second temple, which was referred to as Zerubbabel's temple, was different in structure and splendour from Solomon's temple. Notably, God's physical presence did not descend on the second temple as it did during the dedication of Solomon's temple. Also, the Ark of the Covenant

was no longer available to be put into the Holy of Holies which from that time henceforth remained a dark room. Despite these significant differences between the two temples, the people of Israel were happy and celebrated with joy that their God had returned to live with them. Temple rituals, liturgies, and worship were restored.

The critical functions of the temple including sacrifices, prayer, and a place to receive God's forgiveness, were again on several occasions disrupted with the change of the political history of Israel. It was under the rule of the Syrian King Antiochus IV Epiphanes (175–164 BC) that the temple was again looted and the Jewish culture of sacrifices and circumcision were abolished. The temple was desecrated when a statue of Zeus was placed in the temple and pigs were offered as sacrifices to it. Can God allow this to happen to his house? When God's people become unholy because of sin, God can remove his presence from their midst and turn them over to unholy people. Israel again lost the Lord's presence until Herod built the third temple.

God Meets His People and Lives in Them in the New Testament

Until its destruction in AD 70, the temple remained a critical place in the economic, social, and spiritual life of the people of Israel. After the destruction of Herod's temple, the Jewish people lost the located presence of God. However, Scripture continued to use the temple motif symbolically. The temple was no longer a physical place where God's people would offer animal sacrifices, where God would speak to his people and offer them forgiveness for their sin. But the functions of the temple continued albeit in the spiritual realm. God's presence was not restricted to the temple. The prophet Joel spoke of a time in the future when the Spirit of the Lord will be poured out upon all people (Joel 2:28), sharing God's promise that he will make his home amongst his people in Jerusalem (Joel 3:21). From these two passages we envisage a new temple that will come to be when God's Spirit and glory will live among his people.

One Greater than the Temple

John 1:14 tells us that God himself, through the incarnation, became a human being and dwelt among his people. Jesus Christ, who is called the "radiance of the glory of God" (Heb 1:3, ESV) became the real temple and ultimate place where God met his people. It is worthy to note that the expression John used "and made his home among us" (1:14b) is the same expression used to refer to the tabernacle. Christ is the temple. He paid the ultimate sacrifice for the forgiveness of sins and is our high priest.

The writer to the Jewish Christians in the book of Hebrews drew an interesting parallel between the temple, sacrifices, and Jesus Christ. These Christians were rejecting Jesus Christ and returning to their old Jewish practices because of intense persecution. The writer of the book of Hebrews explains how the Old Testament temple and practices point to Jesus Christ. In chapters nine and ten, the writer indicated that the tabernacle was a replica of heaven itself (Heb 9:23–25) thus, in heaven, we will not need the tabernacle as Christ himself will appear before God on our behalf (Heb 9:24). If the tabernacle were no longer needed, then logically, the sacrifices would no longer be needed as Christ had paid the perfect sacrifice and through the blood of Jesus Christ, "we can boldly enter heaven's Most Holy Place" (Heb 10:19). In effect, the writer of Hebrews was urging people to no longer return to temple worship but to live their lives in total submission to Christ – the perfect temple.

In John 2:18–21, when the Jewish leaders asked Jesus to show a sign that his authority was from God, Jesus replied "Destroy this temple and in three days I will raise it up." "What!" they exclaimed. "It has taken forty-six years to build this Temple and you can rebuild it in three days?" But when Jesus said, "this Temple," he meant his own body. God in Christ Jesus became flesh and lived among his people. There was a significant shift in the understanding of the temple in the gospels. The Gospel of John presents Jesus as the fulfilment of Jewish religious symbols, institutions, and practices to the extent that the physical location of worship had become inadequate and irrelevant and that in Jesus we now find the proper and permanent form of worship.[9] A physical edifice called the temple was no longer needed. A critical function of the temple was reconciliation – God reconciling himself with his people. Christ fulfilled the role of reconciling sinners to God (2 Cor 5:19). He became the high priest – mediating on behalf of his people. Christ had replaced the temple.

For thirty-three years, God's physical presence was with us, consequently, humanity no longer needed a physical space and place to worship God as Christ explained to the Samaritan woman at the well – "when true worshippers will worship the Father in spirit and in truth" (John 4:23). But Jesus being human was limited to a physical location – he could only be at one spot at a time, just like the tabernacle and the temple. Shortly before his death, Christ promised his perpetual presence with us though the Holy Spirit who will

---

9. Kostenberger, Andreas J. *A Theology of John's Gospel and Letters: The Word, the Christ, the Son of God*. Grand Rapids: Zondervan, 2009, 403–435.

indwell the believer (John 16:7). Through the Holy Spirit, God's presence will be with all of humanity. This promise was fulfilled in Acts 2:2–4. The way the Spirit descended on the disciples with "sound from heaven like the roaring of a mighty windstorm, and it filled the house where they were sitting. Then what looked like flames or tongues of fire appeared and settled on each of them" (vv. 2–3) fits the pattern in which the Lord appeared in Exodus 19, Leviticus, 1 Kings 8, and Ezekiel 43. God is now dwelling in us – first in the approximately 120 disciples who were gathered.

We are the Temple

In Hebrews 3, a comparison is made between Moses and Christ in relation to God's house. In verse 6a, it says "but Christ, as the Son, is in charge of God's entire house. And we are God's house." God's house has become God's people (the church), and Christ is in charge. St. Paul expounded on the theme of the church being the temple of God when he wrote to the Corinthians saying, "Don't you realize that all of you together are the temple of God, and the Spirit of God lives in you?" (1 Cor 3:16). In 1 Peter 2:5, the church is described as the "spiritual temple." In Ephesians 2:20–22, Paul also referred to all of God's people as *God's house* and "holy temple" when he wrote:

> So now you Gentiles are no longer strangers and foreigners. You are citizens along with all of God's holy people. You are members of God's family. Together, we are his house, built on the foundation of the apostles and the prophets. And the cornerstone is Christ Jesus himself. We are carefully joined together in him, becoming a holy temple for the Lord. Through him you Gentiles are also being made part of this dwelling where God lives by his Spirit.

Scripture also affirms that the body of a follower of Christ is a temple. Paul also wrote

> Run from sexual sin! No other sin so clearly affects the body as this one does. For sexual immorality is a sin against your own body. Don't you realise that your body is the temple of the Holy Spirit, who lives in you and was given to you by God? You do not belong to yourself. (1 Cor 6:18–19)

In the writings of Paul, the presence of God as a building amongst his people ends on an ominous note. God's presence now has a corporate entity – the Christian community has become the temple.[10]

The temple theme pervades the Revelation of John on Patmos Island. Like Isaiah's vision of heaven in which he saw God, sitting on his throne attended by seraphim singing praises to him (Isa 6:1–3), John also saw heaven in the form of the temple. He records "Then I looked and saw that the temple in heaven, God's tabernacle thrown wide open. . . . The Temple was filled with smoke from God's glory and power. No one could enter the Temple until the seven angels had completed pouring out the seven plagues" (Rev 15:5, 8).

As John was concluding his revelation, he indicated the absence of the temple. John wrote

> The twelve gates were made of pearls – each gate from a single pearl! And the main street was pure gold, as clear as glass. I saw no temple in the city, for the Lord God Almighty and the Lamb are its temple. And the city has no need of sun or moon, for the glory of God illuminates the city, and the Lamb is its light. The nations will walk in its light, and the kings of the world will enter the city in all their glory. Its gates will never be closed at the end of day because there is no night there. And all the nations will bring their glory and honor into the city. Nothing evil will be allowed to enter, nor anyone who practices shameful idolatry and dishonesty – but only those whose names are written in the Lamb's Book of Life. (Rev 21:21–27)

God and the Lamb have become the temple and there was no need for a physical meeting place with God. All of God's people now stand in his presence.

The church – the people who compose the body of Christ and the church building or physical space where Christians meet for worship and fellowship –

---

10. Quast, Kevin. *Reading the Corinthian Correspondence: An Introduction*. Mahwah, New Jersey: Paulist Press, 1994, 30.

has been accepted as the New Testament version of the Old Testament temple to the extent that many now refer to the church as the "temple of God." Having a physical edifice in the name of "church" is a new development in Christendom. The reference of New Testament church did not indicate a building, but a body of Christians. It is therefore ironic to see some congregations spending huge sums of money to put up buildings and to maintain them while they ignore the spiritual health of the congregants who constitute the actual church.

At least as early as Eusebius of Caesarea (c. 260–339), Christian writers referred to Christian places of worship as "divine temples."[11] St. Ambrose of Milan (c. 339–397), in dedicating a church building in Milan, referred to the building as a "temple of God."[12] People do not only have this perception of the church as a temple, but the rendering of the church as the temple is repeated each Sunday morning in some congregations I have visited or of which I am a part. Each Sunday morning as we enter the church, we greet each other and share mutual news until the clergy in charge of worship comes over the loudspeaker and shouts

> The LORD is in His Holy Temple, Let all the earth keep silent before him. Enter into His gates with thanksgiving and His courts with praise. I was glad when they said unto me, Let us go into the house of the LORD. Our feet shall stand within thy gates, O Jerusalem. (Hab 2:20, ESV; Psa 100:4, KJV; Psa 122:1–2, KJV)

11. Eusebius, *Historia Ecclesiastica* 10.4.20, edited by Kirsopp Lake, J. E. L. Oulton, and H. J. Lawlor, 2 volumes. Cambridge, Massachusetts: Harvard University Press, 1926 & 1932, http://www.perseus.tufts.edu/hopper/text?doc=urn:cts:greekLit:tlg2018.tlg002.perseus-grc1:10.4.20.

12. Ambrose, *Epistola* 20.2 (PL 11:307f), *Patrologia Latina*, edited by Jacques-Paul Migne, 217 volumes. Paris: 1844–1864. Specifically, Ambrose refers to a *basilicam* ("basilica") which was dedicated as a church building as a *templum Dei* ("temple of God").

At this pronouncement, the noise level in the church will drop, the focus will be on the altar, and hearts and minds will be engaged for worship because the Lord himself has now come into his own house and his presence has been invoked.

The church, being the temple of God, has some fundamental characteristics. First, the church is built according to God's divine specifications. Moses built the tabernacle according to God's divine plan (Exod 25); Solomon built the temple according to exact specifications given to David (1 Chr 28:11–19). Christ is the architect of the church, building it from its foundation, the cornerstone, and the topmost part of it all according to divine plan. In response to Peter's confession, Christ said "upon this rock I will build my church" (Matt 16:18). The physical structure was not in view; the body of Christ – Christians – was in view. We are his workmanship, and we are God's building. It is important that as we are his body, he has assigned responsibilities to each one of us – responsibilities that will allow the body of Christ to grow, to reach others with the gospel message, and to care for each other.

Second, the magnificent design of the church is seen in the cohesion of all its parts. There is unity of purpose in the church, which shares the same faith, hope, and creed though these may be manifested in several ways. In this light all true believers are one in Christ Jesus. We are carefully joined together in him. Through Christ, all believers become the children of Abraham.

Third, the church, as the body of Christ, has the responsibility of implementing the mission of God in the world. Christ referred to us as the "salt and light" (Matt 5:13–16) of the world, bringing the good news of his saving grace to a society that is in turmoil. Through the life and ministry of the church, people from all over will glorify God. Our testimony to the world that we indeed belong to Christ is the love that will exist in the body of Christ (John 13:35). This love was demonstrated by the early church to the extent that God added to their numbers every day. The temple served the same purpose albeit differently. The presence of the temple served as a testimony of God's might to the heathen nation and Solomon's prayer of dedication was inclusive – that God will hear from heaven and answer the prayers of whosoever will pray toward the temple.

Fourth, both the ministry of the temple and that of the church are illustrated in Ezekiel's dream (Ezek 47). While God's people were in exile in Babylon, God gave a vision of a temple to Ezekiel that would represent God's covenant relationship with his people and his creation through the Messiah that was to come. The prophet dreamt of a river flowing from the altar of the temple into a barren land. As it went down toward the Dead Sea, it brought flourishing life on both sides and when it reached the Dead Sea, it made the salty waters fresh and pure. This is what God wants the church to be – bringing life and spiritual vitality wherever its presence is known.

Fifth, God symbolically dwells in the church in the same way he symbolically dwelt in the tabernacle and in the temple. Paul says, "Don't you realize that all of you together are the temple of God and that the Spirit of God lives in you?" (1 Cor 3:16). Christ, the Son of God, is the head of the church (Eph 1:22) and he lives in us and with us. The church and all Christians are accountable to Christ as he uses his full authority over the church. Christ is the Lord of "this temple" and he assigns different responsibilities to different people in the church.

Though there are significant similarities between the church and the temple, there are some differences that should be noted. First, though we refer to the church as a temple, it is not in the sense of Solomon's temple that was built with inanimate objects like bricks and stone that decayed and perished with time. The church is fashioned with the hands of God and is much alive. It keeps growing and expanding with much vitality. It could also be noted that "temple" is used to describe the place of worship for many other religions like Hinduism, Buddhism and Sikhism. The word "church" is used exclusively to describe Christian places of worship.

Second, though we refer to the church as Christ's temple, the liturgy and rituals of the church are different from those performed in the Jewish temple. The rituals and liturgies of the early church bear much similarity to the synagogue. This is also true of worship forms in some mainline churches. In this regard, the question to contend with is this: If the Christian church (spiritual temple) is holier than and superior to the Jewish temple and the synagogue, why should the church copy the worship forms of the temple and synagogue? There is the argument of continuity between the temple and the church, in which case we would have seen more of the Jewish temple rites within the church than those of the synagogue. The point of focus here is that Jewish temple rituals and liturgies are significantly different from those of the current Holy Spirit temple.

Third, quite unlike the temple that had specially appointed persons to serve as priests, who received sacrifices and offerings from God's people, and who stood in the gap between God and his people, in Christ's church all believers are priests. At the death of Christ, the veil covering the Holy of Holies in the temple was torn into pieces, thereby giving the believer in Christ unfettered access to the throne of mercy. Christ is our high priest, and we no longer need to bring sacrifices to appease God; Christ our Lord has paid the full sacrifice, and we now live under his grace.

Implications for Christian Living

In this chapter, we have examined the theme of our relational God who desires to dwell amongst us. We have traced this theme from God's physical presence in the garden of Eden to his spiritual presence in the life of the believer, and finally to his eschatological presence in the new heavens. We have examined the similarities between the temple, a church (that is, a place of Christian worship), and the church (the body of Christ).

What implications do the temple, its purpose, and its major phases of development have for today's Christians? Foremost, the temple, in all phases of its development and manifestation, is holy and it must be kept that way. The body of Christ as the temple of God must be kept holy because it belongs to God, and God is holy. It was because the children of Israel continued in sin and desecrated the temple that the Lord destroyed it. God can also destroy his habitation if it continues in sin.

Second, we must learn from the nation of biblical Israel which took the worship of God lightly. They went into idolatry and spiritual apathy. They believed that they could bribe God with their offerings and sacrifices while disobeying God and following other gods. Jeremiah confronted this attitude of the leaders where the leaders did despicable things while they sought refuge in the temple (Jer 7:8–15). The church today has the tendency to do the same. Some of us even believe that we earn special favours from God when we do our acts of worship. We have even gone ahead to commercialize Christianity which invariably commercializes the body of Christ. Our leaders are more interested in money than service. We must avoid these tendencies and restore the temple to its legitimate purpose. In Matthew 21:12–14, Jesus reacted vigorously to the commercialization of the temple. He drove away all those who were there to make money; just after that he healed the blind and lame in the temple – Christ restored the critical purpose of the temple. God also can cleanse his church in a manner that will not be desirable.

Third, because our body is part of the temple and God dwells in us, we must value it. If our body is valuable to God, then it must be valuable to us. We must desist from doing activities that devalue our bodies – our work ethics, the observance of sabbath rest, the way we manage stress, and the way we treat others may all be indicators of how we value ourselves as temples. Christ gave us the golden rule (Luke 6:31) "Do to others as you would like them to do to you." The slogan "my body, my choice" is unacceptable to Christians because we are not at liberty to do whatever we wish to do with our bodies.

Fourth, the worship, sacraments, and other functions of the temple typified the coming Messiah and the role he will come to play. The temple typified Christ as the ultimate high priest, and the ultimate sacrifice. As we worship Christ, our minds must be focused on the life, work, and death of Christ as we prepare for his second advent. The church is also described as the bride of Christ. We must comport ourselves to the extent that the groom will not despise us when he comes.

Fifth, if Christ lives in us, we must reflect him in our lives. Solomon's temple was as magnificent as it was expensive because it reflected the glory of God. Our body is expensive and wonderfully made, hence it must reflect the Christ that is in us – not in terms of material things but in living like Christ. Many leaders of the church have missed this point. They argue that God is not poor; consequently, to properly reflect God, one must show flamboyancy of wealth. The prosperity gospel is leaning in that direction with leaders doing everything to acquire wealth to the point of diminishing the presence of Christ in them. We must reflect Christ in his mission, character, and ethos.

Sixth, Christ is the head of his body, and the body is accountable to him. The constituted church is not spiritually answerable to bishops, deacons or overseers. Every member of the body is answerable to Christ. Consequently, our leaders must be answerable to Christ and to the body of Christ. Many times, we see leaders creating family-owned ministries and they become "the-be-all-and-end-all." They control everything and are accountable to no one. This sends the leadership of Christ into oblivion. The temple of God typified in the body of believers must be accountable to Christ – the head of the temple.

It is my prayer that we keep the temple of the Lord pure and holy so that he may find it a worthy place to live in. We must become and remain God's Holy Space.

4

Yeast: The Generative Power of God's Kingdom

Mark Labberton

And again [Jesus] said, "To what should I compare the kingdom of God? It is like yeast that a woman took and mixed in with three measures of flour until all of it was leavened." (Luke 13:20–21)[1]

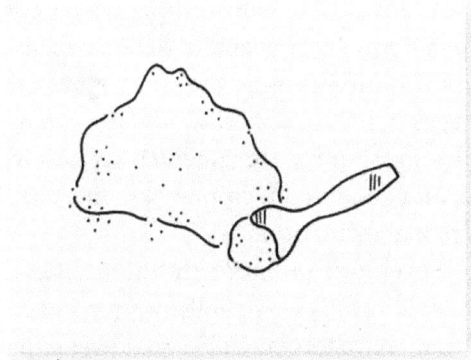

J esus's metaphor of yeast points the church towards the power of its authentic identity, and away from the power that is too often its delusion.

Jesus spoke this metaphor into a world defined primarily by the power of Rome. Astonishingly, that vast and domineering power would in time be subverted by the quiet and invisible gospel of yeast. In the early centuries of

---

1. NRSV, unless otherwise noted all Scripture quotations in this chapter are taken from the NRSV.

Christian faith, the agency of kingdom yeast would also remake assumptions about power and offer in their place the generative power of the reign of God.

Realities of Power

To contextualize the power of God's kingdom yeast, we start with a few reflections about powers that surround and define us wherever we might live. In the first century, as in the twenty-first, people's minds and bodies were defined by facts of power. The personal and public headlines of our modern daily life are also about power. Scan our favourite sources of news, keep track of the verbs of our days, listen to what we ache from or for, and we will see that issues of power are near the core of our memories, pains, joys, and hopes. So much so, that we are preoccupied as finite and vulnerable people with the questions and desires that we believe power has caused or could set right.

We are all affected first by the power of family love and mercy that nurtures and tends us, without which, to some degree, we would not even survive. These can be some of the most defining expressions of power in our lives and, for too many, family can also mean trouble. Our stories can be done and undone by family, and personal relationships throughout our lives include powers that can both build up and tear down. To a baby or infant, a parent contains nearly all forms of power, which frequently expand to the wider family or social context.

Paired with familial power is often the force of formal educational power from the earliest stages of life into adulthood. Our contexts set the possibilities for types of educational influence, in which economic, cultural, religious, political, racialized, and gendered factors will define the limits and hopes of educational and personal formation.

On a biological level, our moment-by-moment existence depends on power. Of course, economically or socially, we readily come to feel we have too little of it, and "they" have too much. So go power dynamics. The strength, nature, and forms of power vary and change over time and context. Meanwhile, facts of actual power within, between, and around us determine so much of life itself. Stories of being human turn around manifestations of power. These are not abstract truisms about power, but the daily experience of every human life.

In the greatest reaches of the universe, the power of suns, moon, stars, and blackholes are themselves defining to our lives. The James Webb Space Telescope takes us in beauty and wonder as close as we have ever been to the start of the universe. At the same time, the complexity and simplicity of genomics open the wonders of our own life's most powerful and personal code. Science develops aspects of gene-based health-care so our bodies receive ever more personalized and effective treatments – unimaginable steps even as we breathe our next breath. Human beings are part of the further and most intimate reaches of the cosmos.

Power has been both the same and radically different over time. The sameness of power over time lies in the human desire for control, and sometimes domination. The differences have come in the force and reach of power. Human power has now cultivated the globe in such ways that we have destroyed our atmosphere. History is the stories of how we have sought to bring nature under human control, but in doing so we have put the whole planet at risk. For evolutionary and ordinary reasons, we sort ourselves, and are sorted sociologically, by factors of power. We are attracted and/or repelled by powers of various sorts. Over time, our sense of contentment reflects how we feel about the sufficiency or insufficiency of our power or the power(s) of others.

What we measure as most relevant to us has to do with the apparent power of some influence or entity we encounter. Fans of various celebrities make this plain every day: their power gives them popularity, and their popularity gives them power. We exercise our own power by identifying with them. We could say the same about ethnic power, economic power, military power, political power, racialized power, sexual power, and so on. Those who ride on underground trains of their city know that just above them is the teeming landscape of the quest and use of power, whether in homes, school, workplaces, social media, or public squares. Our minds can sweep the globe for the mini and meta-narratives of nations caught up in the competitive and sometimes vicious turmoil of twenty-first century powers.

We are living at the moment when, for the first time in history, something humans have made is beginning to control us rather than us fully controlling it: artificial intelligence. The best and the worst outcomes are currently and urgently debatable. What is not debatable is that generative AI already exercises power over our lives, only some of which human beings currently control – and more importantly, only some of which human beings even understand. This is a new power in the world.

This new power unfolds even while the ordinary and pervasive powers of poverty and violence do their brutal work. Local bullies primarily harass and endanger women and children by various acts of emotional, verbal, physical, and sexual violence on any or every given day. They go about destroying the lives of others whom they can control with impunity. Sometimes this power is deployed in forms of human trafficking and slavery, sometimes just for the sheer pleasure of tyranny and domination of others. It may be happening within or among family members where the abuse and sale of their children for exploitation is an ever-increasing crisis.

Through yet another lens, we think of the sixty million global refugees who have been driven away from their homes and nations by religious, political, military, or economic power. Many have the hope of using their power of resilience and intention to find a place of peace, despite their pain and trauma. Caught then in political instability, this leads to more suffering and a context of unending powerlessness. Such refugees are added to the 700 million human beings who live in extreme poverty on less than $2.15/day (USD). Forty-seven percent of the world's population live on less than $6.85/day (USD).

Even with all these powers at play, we search in dismay for reliable powers we do not see sufficiently – powers to: know the truth; stop the madness and pain; bring reliable and sustainable justice; heal; forgive; belong; be fed and housed; love and be loved. Where are these powers? Why are they so difficult to find or to sustain? Amid this writhing combustion of powers, we live our lives – typically in community – while struggling to understand who we are, where we are, and why we matter. Even if we knew those answers, what and where is the power we need to live the answers and questions we hold?

Whether in the first century or our own, daunting powers control peoples' lives. What is astounding, however, is that amid all that is difficult or wrong (not least for those who suffer most) some of what is most right about human beings and the world we inhabit emerges: the powerful presence of beauty and truth, of joy and happiness, of intimacy and love, of grief and death, of creativity and imagination. These are powers for life despite the powers of death. They foster stories of unexpected generativity. They are part of the yeast of God's lifegiving reign.

Yeast and the Kingdom of God

As a poor, first-century Jewish rabbi, Jesus announced that "the kingdom of God is at hand" (Mark 1:15; Matt 3:2; Matt 4:17, ESV).

To be clear: the only evident kingdom at the time was Caesar's, endlessly reasserted and reenforced. To underscore its power in towns in Asia Minor, Rome built (assuredly, by forced labour) magnificent buildings with ornate façades, many feet high, and visible throughout the land. They were not buildings that simply housed a function, mere showpieces; they were signs. Most important and obvious: the building style was about dominance. In the far-flung places in the empire such as Judea – remote and without much of anything, including hope or freedom – Rome made it lavishly and pressingly

clear that it was the dominating presence in that place, towering in might. No distance, expense, or demonstration was too great for Rome.

With full consciousness of this, Jesus announced nothing less than the presence of an alternate and simultaneous kingdom. Its authority was present in Jesus and in his surprising words and actions in public and in private. Jesus showed authority over persons, diseases, nature, religion, and politics, to name a few. He demonstrated power greater than all these, doing so with humility, gentleness, and instruction, rather than domination, militarism, and coercion. He carried unexplained influence which came, he deferred, from his Father, whose will he was seeking to enact. Jesus called the Twelve to follow him, and on the other side of the cross, he gave them "all power and authority" for his kingdom's mission to all the world. His words and deeds embodied an all-encompassing personal and global reign of God's generative love, justice, and mercy through a community of ordinary people. People with changed lives and communities were the monuments Jesus wanted to be seen as evidence of this new kingdom.

In our world of staggering economic, military, technological, and political powers, defining and often destroying millions of lives, people wonder: where is there hope? What kind of power is needed for hope that leads to human and social flourishing and justice? What kind of power understands and honours human beings in all our intense dignity and variety? Is there a power that is about the thriving of each one and of all? In any case, what possible significance can yeast have to such pressing needs? Jesus was never mute before such urgent questions.

The metaphor of yeast was not the first or last time Jesus focused on the unimpressive. Still, let's remember that most bread, beer, and wine, before Jesus's time and still today, are possible because of the single-cells of fungi known as yeast. We may not be all that mindful of them, but they are with us everywhere. These cells live in communities and are found wherever decaying fruit and sugar can be found. Baker's yeast is one kind of yeast among many, many varieties that have valuable properties which cultures have learned to accommodate and deploy for desired outcomes.

As yeast cells do their work, they ingest sugar and release carbon dioxide (CO_2) and ethanol (alcohol). The CO_2 forms air pockets and lifts the dough of the bread and the foam and alcohol of the wine and beer. It is the fruit of their work that makes yeast cells known to us, when they are otherwise, more or less, invisible and unimpressive. Through their permeating and underwhelming presence, they demonstrate highly generative and transformative power.

Into the earthly kingdom of Rome comes Jesus of Galilee. Yeast in his own right. He announces to all who would hear, "The kingdom of heaven is at hand. Repent and believe." (Mark 1:15 ESV) His healing acts and unexpected words about the reign of God caused growing throngs of disciples and followers to hope he was the Messiah who would throw off Roman domination. Performing miracles and speaking in parables and metaphors, Jesus announces that the kingdom of heaven is like a mustard seed, or like yeast inside measures of flour. At a time when Rome had ferociously defined power, and when Israel longed for the Messiah who would overthrow Rome's defeating rule, Jesus declared the presence of another kind of kingdom. With gentle but unflinching confidence, Jesus announced into the public square the arrival of a kingdom of an entirely different order. Amid the Roman power of prominence and domination, Jesus says that God reigns like the subtle, invisible, catalytic, and utterly transformative power of yeast. God's kingdom is not like Caesar's.

Underwhelming. Ludicrous. Irrelevant. Unsuspectingly, Jesus points to an ordinary home where an ordinary woman mixes the ordinary ingredients of leavened bread – where yeast changes, enlivens, and transforms. Such is the nature of God's kingdom. The ministry of Jesus reflects this understated catalytic transformation. It shifts the definitions or expectations of power. It is the stuff of salt and light, seeds and lanterns. It is healing without public fanfare and a Roman centurion's faith exceeding that of Israel. It is seen when Jesus draws in the dirt before an adulterous woman and the law is recast by love. It is demonstrated when the prodigal is embraced by the father. It is most powerful when death is replaced by resurrection. The kingdom of God is unexpectedly generative.

First, in appearance and quality, the kingdom of God as yeast comes to us as something small, insignificant, and undervalued. To announce its presence, let alone its importance, can seem preposterous, if not insulting, when spoken into the bracing winds of pain and the struggles of poverty, violence, abuse, injustice. The darkness will overwhelm anything that seems abstract or naïve. It can feel indulgent even, like news of a successful chess match in a war zone.

In fact, when Jesus used the metaphor of the yeast, it may have felt even more humble and plain. But it turns out that mere yeast, understood truly, can be lifegiving and transformative. What can yeast do with flour that is like what the kingdom of God can do in our lives? The reign to which Jesus points is that of a God who infuses people with the yeast of transformative life. The Lord, who in love created and sustains our aching world, is invisibly but relentlessly kneading in the yeast of our healing and recreation in Jesus Christ "that we might have life, abundantly."

Admitting that throughout history the church at times has seemed, and still seems, to be a lifeless bunch of flour or an inert lump of doubt, it can be vigorously argued that the yeast Jesus refers to is relentlessly at work – but as yeast, not as dynamite, nor as an air pump. It is worked into individual lives invigorating people, circumstances, actions, and possibilities that might otherwise be lifeless. Even so, yeast can also die.

Starting with the first-century disciples themselves, the witness of the four gospels relay as much. From lives of fishermen to preachers, leaders, thinkers, and evangelists – all because of the yeast of Jesus's life, death, resurrection, and Spirit. No surrounding forces were supporting or cheering their efforts, only dangers and threats. Plenty of their own internal confusion or doubt could have subverted or stopped them, but their story did not stop. It expanded far beyond imagining. Life itself was found in and among them. Neither Jesus's death, nor the persecution subsequent to it, could stop the life-resurrecting implications of trusting and living in the reign of God's love.

Some get stopped in their consideration of these circumstances, especially since there is never a shortage of death, injustice, or pain – inside or outside the church. Meanwhile, the witness of Jesus is the generativity of unlikely life in the midst of death. What is this yeast of life in the face of death that, during the worst plagues in the fourth century, caused Christians to be the ones to stay in beleaguered cities and love those who were sick and dying? What is the ingredient in God's yeast that has enabled hundreds, thousands, and millions to see one another as bearers of God's image and entitled to freedom and justice beyond human tyranny and injustice in the rule of law and education?

Sara Miles was raised as a daughter of vehemently faith-rejecting parents who had been children of missionaries. For her, faith was non-existent, and Sara's secular life as a liberal U.S. journalist in Latin America simply carried no sign of its heritage in her family. One unsuspecting day in San Francisco, home on leave and out for a walk, she noticed some fairly large and brightly-painted figures through the clear glass windows of a building she was passing. The doors were open so she wandered in for a closer look. Sitting down to take it all in, she found herself in a small Christian worship service. With others, she found herself synchronously dancing under the belfry with the iconic saints now above her, standing in a tight mosh-pit of diverse San Franciscans gathered around a tall standing table. Without faith and much explanation, and with no anticipation, Sara Miles says she simply found herself suddenly clear about something unimaginable and unassailable: "God was in her mouth." The yeast utterly changed her life. She now serves as a priest in that Anglican congregation (St. Gregory's) and established one of San Francisco's largest food pantries that serves food to the poorest people as a manifestation of the "yeast" of the Lord's table.[2]

As Jesus teaches and exemplifies, yeast is enemy-love. Yeast is going two miles, not just one. Yeast is touching the untouchable. Yeast is eating at the table of sinners. Yeast is healing on the sabbath. Yeast is a few fish and loaves feeding a large crowd. Yeast is laying down self-interest for the sake of love over dominance. Yeast is kingdom life in action amid the vulnerable and the ordinary. Yeast permeates and brings alive what is otherwise inert. Yeast is the catalyst of Jesus's life, death, and resurrection doing what no one and nothing else can do.

Then and now, this humble metaphor captures the unexpected and peculiar power of God's reign. As Jesus anticipated, this portrait of the power of God's kingdom has never been popular. The personal and collective vulnerability of those over whom Rome dominated, wanted nothing less than regime change – and that surely called for aggressive, visible power battles with public defeat of the enemy and public success of the victor. But that was not, and is not, the way of Jesus. Throughout the four gospels, in the calling of his disciples Jesus embodied the way of yeast. Even in his final words, Jesus entrusted the mission of God's people to eleven (not twelve) believer-doubters: yeast, on good days. Yeast kneaded into flour is all.

Church: A Communion of Rightly-Ordered Power

Jesus taught unflinchingly that power is central to the reign of God. This is why Jesus started and finished his earthly ministry defining the distinct character, evidence, and purpose of God's power through Jesus, and then through the life of the church by the power of the Holy Spirit. Jesus was, and is, com-

2. Miles, Sara. *Take This Bread*. New York: Ballentine Books, 2008.

mitted to reordering power for the sake of a new and healing kingdom. The primary Christian confession – "Jesus is Lord" – plainly personalizes and underscores this. However, the power of God's reign is not portrayed as that of a conquering victor but as God's self-emptying personal sacrifice. From the moment of Peter's confession that Jesus is the Christ, and since Jesus chose to move towards public crucifixion, and from when the disciples learned they must in turn lay down their own lives, Jesus's vision for sacrificial power has largely been a bitter pill for the church.

In the book of Acts, and the rest of the New Testament letters, we are given immediate and proximate images of how the church began to live into its identity. It began with waiting three days and Jesus's resurrection from the dead (power never before seen). Next came Jesus's Great Commission with ministry and power given to eleven believer–doubters. Then the Holy Spirit arrived like fire and rushing wind, with unexpected speech, on the day of Pentecost, and Peter proclaimed the good news by which 3,000 believed and were baptized. All of this was public evidence and fruitfulness of the kingdom of God, though by unseen power and mystery.

In some ways, the writings of the New Testament are all about the interactions of power – religious, political, social, ethnic, gender, generational, and more. We see this in the disciples' struggles to understand and imitate Jesus, to be open to the instruction of the Holy Spirit who calls Saul and welcomes Gentiles (not Jews only) and who creates communities of believers that are not sorted by any of the typical lines of separation in first-century Palestine and beyond. The collisions over power between the Roman Empire and the apostles, and particularly Peter and Paul, are defining parts of the New Testament. Paul's seeking the chance to speak before Caesar in Rome, without fear because of the kingdom power within him, underlines the moment and the trajectory for a gospel-shaped reordering of power.

When Peter cut off the ear of the Roman soldier arresting Jesus, he seemed fully convinced that was the way to act – until Jesus rebuked him for using such aggression to try to stop the arrest, and then healed the man's ear. Psychologically, Jesus's counterintuitive approach cuts across the protective lines of self-defence, that is, fear is presumably what directed Peter's sword, but Jesus was redefining fear altogether. Having determined to live with freedom from fear (including fear of death), Jesus was free to engage in his trial and even his crucifixion in generative ways despite all pressures to the contrary.

One can readily take a simple look at the early history of the church up to today and see many earnest efforts to follow Jesus's model and instruction. Over the millennia and around the globe, faithful Christians and congregations have lived according to Jesus's freedom by pursuing acts of love, righteousness, and justice. Towns, societies, and nations have been changed by this kind of faithful yeast, bringing life to places marked by death. Contemporary examples include the Black church in South Africa bringing an end to apartheid, and the Black church in the United States in redefining practices of justice. Even so, there are many ways the church is prone to align or mimic the ways of empire rather than to follow the understated ways of Jesus's self-emptying power. What Jesus did and how he lived is part of the yeast of an entirely new kingdom. The church has often tended towards believing it can make power better, when Jesus says we need to demonstrate power that is new, not of the same material.

We have the great and historic Christian traditions: Roman Catholicism, Eastern Orthodoxy, Anglicanism, Protestantism, Pentecostalism. These can appear to be monoliths, matrices, or both. Their towering edifices often convey a decaying grandeur of vision for God and for the faith. To passers-by, they are like the vestiges of outdated, visual furniture in the urban or rural landscape, not a living and urgently needed source of life. They can seem like boxes of ecclesiastical religion, caged off in their own irrelevant universe. They are the signs of what perhaps once was but is no longer for so many, a world irrelevant to someone defined by today's language, crises, appetites, and yearnings.

We can scan our horizon for church buildings (or billboards, websites, conferences, TV programming, movies, and more) that stand up like those ancient Roman edifices to announce the church's prominence. The picture is complex and easily disillusioning. Seen from one angle, the pervasive scandals of the church's past and present reveal rank and protected abuses of power of so many kinds and in so many places: gender abuse, sexual abuse, ethnic abuse, racist abuse, economic abuse, political abuse are just some. These are not limited to a denomination or a region of the world but are ubiquitous everywhere that the church is found. Whether hierarchical structures or individual leaders, the wrong extends deep and wide. "A few bad apples" simply does not stem the disillusionment and moral offence. While these are examples of over-reaching power, the void of power the church displays cannot seem to address the church's own ills or present evidences of lifegiving power to hold social despair in check or to offer realistic hope in a world where powers of various sorts are ruining lives.

So many youth and young adults are looking for real hope that will require freedom and confidence in trustworthy power. Often that is through some kind of social influence, money, power, or brand. It is varied around the world, nuanced by culture and access to resources, fostered by creativity. It assumes that the social realities for young adults puts the questions of identity, belonging, and purpose on the line every day, both for themselves, and for those at the margins who need justice. Institutions are suspected or rejected in exchange for the immediate, the communal, the honest, the authentic, the egalitarian, the next.

Five Qualities of Yeast to Reorder Power in the Twenty-First Century Church: Humility, Integrity, Equity, Unity, and Love
1. In an Arrogant World, the Yeast of Jesus's Power Comes in Humility

The global ecclesiastical industrial complex presents the most visible and vocal part of the church. This easily suggests that its form and size constitute the church's power. The church itself can believe this delusion. By contrast, Jesus's humility shuns display and especially the trumpeting of his miracles. Understatement and simplicity are far more the way of Jesus. The plainness of yeast masks its capacity to transform. The resurrection is the most dramatic of Jesus's actions, and yet it happens at dawn in an insignificant tomb.

When the church shows up in the world in humble lives of the saints, ancient and modern, they display in word and action that Jesus's kingdom is not about competition, winning, or dominance. It is about listening, caring, serving. It is about accompaniment in places of pain and need. Jesus repudiates Satan's first temptation to him in the wilderness by refusing Satan's offer to give him all the power on earth.

The history of the church is both a story of thriving transformation and of self-inflicted pockmarks from betraying its true life. In rethinking the church's identity and life, none of its past can be denied, but that also means naming the wonderous vitality of the church, despite all odds, alongside the church's brokenness. The humility of yeast holds the full dimensions of the church. It was, for example, the church that served with risk and sacrifice those who were sick and dying from the Black Plague. This was embodying the quiet, generative, if counterintuitive, presence of Jesus's love and compassion in hidden spaces and lives. While colonizing influences of the church brought many devastating consequences, it also brought an affirmation of human dignity that still undergirds human rights around the world.

When church leaders have chosen to live in humility before God and before their neighbours, including their enemies, that surprising, permeating quality reorders their power and the powers they affect. Pope John Paul XXIII, Dorothy Day, Bishop Oscar Romero, Mother Theresa, and Father Greg Boyle are all recognizable exemplars of such yeast. Pope Frances shocked the curia with simple gestures of welcoming kindness towards children, touching those of poor reputation or infectious disease, and making unanticipated personal confession in public view. His life and engagement are signs of generative hope, even when internal church forces push back.

When the Pope, on the other hand, has seemed slow to lead the accountability of priests at all levels of ecclesial ranks, then the questions of *what power* arise again – where is the humility? the honesty? Most often those inside or outside the church do not think humility is generative yeast, but when it is present, it leaves an authenticating mark of credibility, typically without attention.

We seek a clear estimate of ourselves and the church as measured by the humble sacrifice and redemptive offering of Jesus described in Philippians 2. The current state of the church in places around the world makes this an urgent season for practicing personal and corporate church humility before God and before one another. This would ideally embrace such spiritual practices as silence, confession, lament, repentance, and prayer. An altar call, as it were, for people to face the God who reigns in humility, and who urges us to bow before the One who alone is Lord. As individuals and as communities, we must do an honest and candid assessment of the faith and faithlessness of the church, and of our individual and collective pride.

Variations in Christian traditions, hierarchies, liturgies, and practices will approach this differently. By remembering the plainness of yeast, let us encourage ourselves and one another to be as plainspoken and frank in naming the hypocrisies, idolatries, and pride that have so exposed our failure to live as faithful disciples, siblings, and witnesses. Our self-interested tendency towards chasing power and influence for our own sake or for our institution or movement's sake reveals that the yeast of God's kingdom is not what permeates our life. The church all too often does not look like the Jesus we claim to imitate.

Humility empowers the kind of generative courage to live and speak out in contexts of competing and colliding power. By the goodness and creativity of God, we are meant to grow in humility to embrace and embody a true understanding of ourselves in relation to God, ourselves, and our neighbours. Rather than taking a posture of self-defence and over-reach, practicing a humble Christian identity allows us to live in freedom and sacrifice more than competition. Within the diverse body of Christ, we form a communion that emerges from Christ's death and resurrection. Highly diverse people are knit into God's new humanity where each person finds themselves drawn into a community of humility kneaded together as one. The generative impact of God's yeast transforms our lives into a common life for the sake of others.

Christian character, embodied together, redefines what it means to live in a world of arrogant tyranny and injustice. The church can then authentically step into challenging realities with realism and freedom, knowing consequences are in God's hands, and that generative hope is to be the church's lifestyle.

2. In an Imaged-World, the Yeast of Jesus's Power Comes in Integrity

We live in a world where images have less and less to do with reality. Artificial Intelligence creates and spreads images as we work and as we sleep. It finds, grabs, manipulates, algorithmically plunders, and distributes images everywhere. It is all part of creating the imaged-world you and I call life in the twenty-first century. These realities define more than we know, so we are often sceptical or dismissive about images, but we are hooked by and dependent on them all the same. Human beings have never been more thoroughly "seen" than today when appearance can be all.

The kingdom of God values integrity – the inner and outer embodiment of character and compassion – that is, incarnation means living what we profess. Integrity is present when what appears to be true is true and is true to the core. The scandal that "the Word became flesh" (John 1:14) in Jesus is the embodiment of integrity. In part, it is evidence of God's integrity. If we want to know what the invisible God is like, look at Jesus – whose life, words, and deeds show us the integrity of God's being. In part, the incarnation is also evidence of human integrity, when what Jesus says and what he does are wholly consistent. Integrity.

In Jesus's yeast metaphor yeast is a single-cell fungus that is worked into the three scoops of flour, and then left to fully be and become its full self, thoroughly diffused and integrated, alongside a measure of water and salt. As it sits in a bowl at the proper temperature, the yeast thrives and infuses the flour until the dough is ready to be baked. Plain ingredients, mixed, and manifest in a loaf with all its integrity and vitality. In the simplest of terms, the dough (and the baked loaf) is thoroughly and only itself. It does not carry a promise to be bread, only to turn out to be a wrench or a bomb.

Human integrity is never going to match the integrity of Jesus Christ. If that was the earthly goal, Jesus would not have commissioned eleven believer-doubters (Matt 28) to carry forth the mission of his reign. The church will never be perfect. What is realistic and expected is that the church be credible – that what Christians claim about life in Christ is consistent with how they speak and act. Plain ingredients, mixed, transformed so the church can be itself through and through.

Yet, the Lord warned long ago that God's people are no less image-oriented than their neighbours; at times, the church still shows more interest in its image than in reflecting the reality of God's image in the world. Living today in an already image-drenched world, AI is taking the apparent to far greater extremes. AI may not yet be perfect in its efforts, but it is already more than enough to make distinguishing between the real and the apparent problematic. Symbolically and tangibly, a dramatic move towards becoming an even more imaged-world makes the need for, and the challenge of, incarnation all the greater. This is a critical part of how the church's identity needs most to be reaffirmed and rediscovered. God's people are to be the living enactment of God's loving, just reign for the individual and for the community. The church is to be a credible witness to God. The all-too-frequent failure in the integrity of the church is its own downfall. Kingdom yeast is God's unexpected means of that reversal.

We seek to be a church with integrity – a self-consistency of being and doing that credibly reflects the reality of God's yeast in God's people. The permeating presence of yeast is demonstrated in the risen dough. We recognize its generative influence by its integrity. To be a church like this requires humility to yield to the kneading impact that thoroughly and deliberately works the yeast into all of the flour. This is the work of the Holy Spirit working with the critical ingredients. The simplicity of Jesus's metaphor emphasizes the presence of what is needed, and by implication, the absence of what does not belong. So too, the life of the church fundamentally requires only simple elements.

The church, in all of its ecclesiastical industrial size, diversity, and complexity, tells a wildly different story. While yeast is by no means the only image

Jesus used for the reign of God, and the narrative of Jesus is more complex, the integrity of the church as God's generative power can never be less than or other than these simple ingredients. This is the life in which the church knows and shows itself. The spiritual, liturgical, organizational, missional being of the church demonstrates its integrity only as far as the yeast of God's kingdom is present and active.

Integrity of this sort is itself a work of God's grace so, strictly speaking, God is the giver and maintainer of the church's integrity. As with any form of faithful human stewardship of God's gifts, Jesus and the rest of Scripture instruct the church to order its life and power in ways that are measured by God's integrity and wisdom. The all-too-frequent practice of the church has been to focus more on its own systems and structures, its appearance, than on the central life and integrity of God which it is to manifest. Increased layers of tradition, form, habits, assumptions, and idols create a practical distance between God's life and the institutional life of the Church. We seek a clear estimate of ourselves and the church as measured by the humble sacrifice and redemptive offering of Jesus described in Philippians 2. The current state of the church in places around the world makes this an urgent season for practicing personal and corporate Christian humility before God and before one another. This would ideally embrace such spiritual practices as silence, confession, lament, repentance, and prayer. An altar call, as it were, for people to face the God who reigns in humility, and who urges us to bow before the One who alone is Lord. As individuals and as communities, we must do an honest and candid assessment of the faith and faithlessness of the church, and of our individual and collective pride before God and one another.

Variations in Christian traditions, hierarchies, liturgies, and practices approach this differently by remembering individual lives and the institutional life of the church. Too often, however, form supplants being and appearance supplants doing hence the cry throughout history of the problems of hypocrisy. The church's only life is its yeast, kneaded throughout the flour.

In the current crises facing the church, many voices point to other materials, other mediums, other technologies as the hope of the church. "Giving the people what they want" and imitating culture were seldom Jesus's strategies, but they are too frequently the church's inclination. Of course, the church is meant to see and engage its own needs and those of the surrounding world. But when the church loses its clarity and fails to demonstrate that the integrity of God's faithful love, mercy, and justice is our life and our mission, the church will tend to mimic culture while it surrenders its true hope. Personal and corporate intentionality, and dependence on the Holy Spirit, is central to rethinking church.

Seeking and practicing Christian integrity is within the grasp of any disciple, not perfectly but credibly. Every believing person or community faces their own challenges in living this out, but it is to be our daily bread to do so. We seek to tell the truth, to do what we say, to see and love with compassion and justice, especially those who are most vulnerable. When congregations demonstrate this internally and externally, everyone realizes something distinctive and substantial is present. It is faithful yeast generatively at work.

3. In an Unjust World, the Yeast of Jesus's Power Comes with Equity

As plain as the image of yeast is, there is also a striking absence of hierarchy. This may push the limits of the metaphor, of course, but it comes in such contrast to the dominant hierarchies of Rome, and of religious and other powers of Jesus's day. The yeast becomes equitably pervasive in the flour or the wine. The success of kneading the dough or stirring the vat of wine is to seek full and thorough distribution of the yeast so its effects are everywhere. The baker's success requires this equity.

Struggles for power among the first disciples continued from their first call to be with Jesus, up to and beyond his death and resurrection. Jesus's ministry demonstrates that his reordering of power was not and is not oriented towards the powerful but towards the needy, which includes the powerful. Again and again, Jesus's example calls the disciples to live into a new kingdom that includes strangers, foreigners, enemies, and sinners all. The readiness of Jesus to extend the healing and grace he offered clashed with the religious, political, and social boundaries of power all around him. Jesus was scandalously expansive and equitable in sharing all he had to give. The public standing of Jairus and the urgency of his sick daughter did not hinder Jesus from stopping for the woman with a twelve-year flow of blood. This yeast is for all.

The human deference to hierarchies of power has always been evident in the life of the church. As the ministry of the body of Christ spread, with gifts of greater and lesser prominence yet of equal value, the temptations to perpetuate hierarchies of power is seen in many New Testament texts (e.g. the gospels, Galatians, Acts, 1 and 2 Corinthians). Reordering power is part of the work of the Holy Spirit to make the church show forth the dying and rising that is the evidence of God's "new humanity" (Eph 2:15). Where the church has lived this authentically and progressively, the power of such equity has been transformative inside and outside the church.

The declining power of the church around the world triggers some in Christian leadership to seek and assert power that looks much more like its surrounding cultures. Jesus never advocated that strategy. Instead, in broken-ness and weakness, this season in the church's life is an opportunity to reorder the power that is meant to produce an equitable embodiment of the reality of God's capacious grace and truth.

It is an understandable perplexity that the church has been inclined to mirror hierarchies of power rather than to mimic the kenotic life of Jesus (Phil 2:5–9), "who, though he was in the form of God, did not regard equality with God as something to be exploited, but emptied himself, taking the form of a slave, being born in human likeness . . ." (vv. 6–7). It was also Jesus who pointed with essential and hierarchical deference to "the Father" whose will alone was Jesus's mission and purpose. Worship cultivates a life of humble deference to God supremely and uniquely. The "keys" that Jesus gives to the church are keys of authority defined and demonstrated by the humility of Jesus in relation to the Father.

In time, over years and centuries of hierarchical roles and structures defin-ing the Roman and Eastern churches, divine authority and power has been understood to be in the hands of those who bear an apostolic vocation. The fifteenth-century "Doctrine of Discovery" gave church explorers and emissaries the authority to take control of the lands and peoples they encountered. This led to a church hegemony that still affects the lives of colonized Indigenous People around the world, even if recently withdrawn by the Pope. These assumptions of church authority contributed to the Protestant Reformation which believed that the Bible was its own authority and that anyone and everyone should have access and freedom to read the Scriptures themselves to hear the Word of God and to respond accordingly. While this by no means led to an easy or common equity in the body of Christ, it led to developments where true equity can be imagined.

Rethinking equity in the church for the twenty-first century requires facing the inequities in the ways the church has ordered its life in relation to women, children, ethnicities, classes, economics, education, and more. Neither high-church nor low-church Christians have consistently demonstrated the universal equality of humans made in the image of God and ordered church for the sake of the flourishing of all. This is not an abandonment or rejection of faithful and appropriate hierarchy, but a tangible accountability to the equity of God's creative and redeeming love and justice.

The protracted and tragic abuses of power in the life of the church and its mission scandalize the gospel and repel moral people across the world.

If the church cannot translate this essential quality into reordered life, then the claim to be the yeast of God's kingdom is fraudulent and coercive. This urgent reparative work is not done in imitation of secular cultures or religious hegemonies, but in imitation of the life and love of Jesus whose yeast is meant to reorder power of all kinds.

4. In a Divided World, the Yeast of Jesus's Power Comes in Unity

The nature of yeast is a unifying image. Successful use of yeast assumes unity. The assumption of oneness is inherent and fundamental. The same is true of Jesus's vision for the people of God. Ephesians 4 captures it this way: "there is one body and one Spirit, just as you were called to the one hope of your calling, one Lord, one faith, one baptism, one God and Father of all, who is above all and through all and in all" (vv. 4–6).

What makes this vision particularly remarkable is the way that the ministry of Jesus and of the early apostles unfolded in context of conflicting diversity across ethnicity, religion, gender, and more. The church is to be a manifestation of a united community of unlike people. In fact, the church is meant to authenticate the death and resurrection of Jesus by this otherwise unexplainable communion. This reordering of competing powers through the communion centred in one God – Father, Son, and Spirit – is meant to be the living experience and witness of the church. The church finds its unity in the mediator, Jesus Christ, not in one another (by looking through dividing sociological hierarchies and differences), nor by centring on the church (as a mediating institution which has so often failed to reorder beyond its confession that Jesus is Lord).

No wonder this theme of unity has played into assumptions of hierarchy, bureaucracy, and monolith. While those expressions of institutionalized unity are understandable, their prominence has supplanted a unity created and sustained by the inwardly unifying life of the Holy Spirit.

The church can only be renewed by the Holy Spirit when it experiences the shared and unifying life of God in Jesus Christ. The church is first and foremost meant to find its life and express its power through this unity in which individuals can become ever more like Christ and therefore ever more fully themselves for the other. It is a generative and capacious unity, not a closed and privileged circle. Its unity naturally leads to seeking the inclusion of those outside it. Out of God's love, the church exists for the sake of those outside it.

In a global church of 45,000 denominations, unity can hardly be shown to be a priority of the church across time or around the world. The unity of the church is principally the unity of the Triune God, made possible through the perfect communion of the Father, the Son, and the Holy Spirit. It is a community-in-and-with the One God. This means a unity of being and doing in Jesus Christ, not principally of form and structure.

In reclaiming and embodying the nature of the kingdom's yeast, the unity of the church is not an idea but a living communion of unlike people who hold in common the permeating influence of God's yeast as it makes us alive together. This is a communion in vulnerability and dependency. We are held in this communion by the living reality of God's love, and the capacity to overcome the death that isolates us from God and one another. We pursue then a unity of being and doing that is God's generative life, which defeats in his death and resurrection forces within and between us that divide and separate rather than unite us. Jesus is the mediator in all relationships and the church lives through the perpetual habit of seeing one another through him.

Calvin saw the church as a schoolhouse in which we practice in each other's presence our new humanity emerging out of a new communion. This must be both explicit and an implicit modus operandi – all of the other habits of our life and faith are meant to be held in this way. This is why Jesus's words in the Sermon on the Mount call forth a comprehensively different world and communion that reflects the yeast of the kingdom.

In a polarized era, where the church shows itself to be politically, ideologically, and ecclesiastically divided, the absence or wreckage of unity subverts the identity and mission of the church. It is not regained by organizational restructuring but by living into the life of God's love that draws us into a true communion in difference.

Rethinking unity only matters as we respond to one other out of a desire to love one another beyond the sociology we are handed by society. It takes practice, individually and collectively, to choose to perceive, name, and act towards one another because of the gospel-yeast that we share in common.

5. In a Violent World, the Yeast of Jesus's Power Comes with Love

The power of violence defines much of the natural world and is everywhere present throughout the pages of the Bible. It is all over the world. Its destruction is rampant and global. It manifests in ways that are vivid and stealthy. It defined Jesus's day and our own.

The yeast of the kingdom of God points to the making of bread that is fundamentally nourishing to family and friends, and even to enemies. It is an expression of hospitality and kindness. It gives a gift that every culture seeks and needs, and therefore receives as an assured good. Everyone requires food and water, and bread is one of the most basic cultural expressions of filling that need. Nothing about bread is violent or destructive. In fact, Jesus portrays yeast being incorporated into flour by a woman in a home as an ordinary, gentle act of love.

This is perhaps *the* unspoken but underlying essence of the yeast image. With no agency of its own, the kneader or baker folds and incorporates the yeast into the flour, that becomes the dough, which becomes the bread. Love activates the yeast. This is not the power of the bureaucrat or of their institution. It is the work of people, God's people, in a world starving for love. This underscores context, intentionality, care, and vulnerability. Though breadmaking has long since industrialized, the image Jesus uses is not about scale. It is about what happens around a table or near a hearth, face-to-face, hand-to-hand.

Love is most tangibly present where the church shows itself to be profoundly transformative. The lifegiving love of family and friends, of neighbours and acquaintances, of teachers and coaches is hand-to-hand. It is close and personal. None of today's best technology is required because those things are not the essence of what life is or requires. In Jesus's image, yeast is nothing without love.

As the church grew from its tiny start to now including more than two billion people across the globe, it imitated all the tools and principles of organizations and structures with their confessions, hierarchies, divisions of labour, liturgies, and practices. Most often the church claims what it does is done in the name of *love*. How the church structures and orders itself seems to be about *power*. Is this a contradiction? Yes, when power is primary, and love merely greases the wheels of bureaucracy. Yes, too, when power overwhelms or marginalizes love, or when love is treated as an ecclesial reward rather than a constituting gift from God. When love is merely an institutional gesture, it is not intrinsic or primary to releasing the transformative power of yeast. But are the two always in conflict? No, not if the church lives its life faithfully.

Today, institutional church power is in global decline – and, as in the past, that may be a gift. In such a time, instincts can quickly move towards nostalgia and recovery, however, rather than towards repentance, lament, confession, and renewal. Love motivates the latter, and historical power wants the former. The future of the church does not primarily depend on bureaucratic improvement. It depends on the rediscovery and alignment with the life and love of God that reorders power: the yeast of the kingdom of God.

The global ecclesiastical industrial complex presents the most visible and vocal part of the church. This easily suggests that its form and size constitute the church's power. The church itself can believe this delusion. When the church commits itself to such outcomes over the invisible and subtle power of God's life in and through it, it is like promoting the appearance of bread, or the bottle that holds the wine. That strips the church of its authentic witness to God's transformative life. It can mean the church offers the people forms of Christian religion rather than its living essence. Such a church is inauthentic to God and to itself. No wonder it becomes so for so many others as well.

The yeast of God's kingdom is the life of the church, a fundamental fact that cannot change. When the church forgets or neglects this in its striving after other powers, or in imitation of those powers rather than the life of God in Christ, the church empties itself of what is most important, authentic and sustaining. It is certainly true that ecclesial forms can lead us to God's life, but when "the method is the message," spiritual bankruptcy has often been the result. This is how yeast can be killed.

The most impressive power of kingdom yeast is God's unexplainable and inextinguishable love. This is not just the exegetical, credal, and liturgical verbalizations of love primarily, but the private and public embodiment of love that conveys life to the dead. It is the incarnational manifestation of the exegetical, creedal, and liturgical verbalizations of love that is the gospel.

This love requires no money, building, or structure. It is like yeast. It is understatedly given and kneaded through compassion, mercy, presence, and persistence. The immediacy and accessibility of love involves the power of human agency arising from the heart. It is not sentimentality, but about seeing, hearing, and responding to another human being. Our capacities for this are ones we "catch" from our families and friends, that we receive and return. Our development occurs as we grow up experiencing some degree of hearth through relationships, food, education, work.

It is as people of faith, with the added privilege of love that is not given or received because of bloodlines or tribes, similarities or differences. Rather, a

love that is the yeast of God's love in which we find ourselves most profoundly known and seen, in our life and in our death, in which "nothing can separate us from the love of God."

The hope that is the church lies in it living its identity. Yeast is but one of the defining pictures of who we are to be and how we are to live the distinctive life of the kingdom of God. Sorting out the images of power that have confused and distracted the church is a never-ending process. Rethinking the images that Jesus gave us to know God and to know ourselves is the pathway to the unexpectedly generative life of God's reign demonstrated through God's people. These simple words point to the way forward: humility, integrity, equity, unity, and love. May we receive the yeast of God's kingdom individually and collectively, and let it do its generative work in and through ordinary people and congregations. If we do so, it will be a witness to the profound hope and transformative power that Jesus meant for his people to show, especially in a world of disordered powers.

5

The People of God: Together in Tribulation

Oscar Jiménez

But you are a chosen clan, a royal priesthood, a holy nation, a *people* for God's possession, that you may declare the praises of him who called you out of darkness into his wonderful light. *Once you were not a people, but now you are the people of God*; once you had not received mercy, but now you have received mercy. (1 Pet 2:9–10, NIV[1])

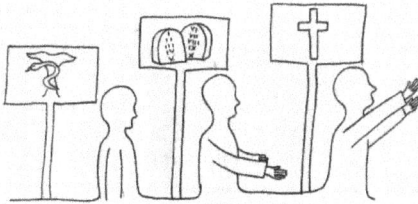

---

1. All Scripture translations presented in entirely italics are those of the author; other biblical passages quoted are taken from the New International Version (NIV). Portions of biblical passages from the NIV highlighted in *italics* represent my emphasis.

Step with me on a journey that dives into the challenges and blessings of immigration today. In the following pages, you will discover how believers – no matter their ethnic, cultural, and social backgrounds – can unite and see themselves as a cohesive movement, due to their shared bond as God's chosen people. By revisiting the inspiring story of Israel in the Old Testament, we will uncover how the identity of God's chosen people bridges the gap between the early believers of Peter's time and us today. As our journey culminates, we will uncover the profound relevance that the metaphor "people of God" holds for both immigrant communities and those who see themselves as spiritual exiles within their own land.[2]

Immigration Today

In today's increasingly interconnected world, the journey of immigration weaves a rich tapestry of emotions and experiences. The number of people forced to leave their homes worldwide is estimated to have been 117.3 million by the end of 2023. This number is up 8% from 2022, and it is over double the amount in 2014. This statistic is record breaking: 43.4 million refugees and 68.3 million internally displaced people (those who sought refuge within their own country after fleeing their homes).[3] According to the 2021 census, one in six people then living in Wales and England was born outside of the UK; approximately half a million of these were refugees.[4]

As the global community continues to expand, immigrants encounter the complexities of living in another place as strangers: displacement, disorienta-

---

2. In this chapter, I explore the metaphor "people of God," focusing on its relevance for the contemporary church's understanding of its identity and mission. This question inevitably influences the project's starting point and, to a certain extent, my engagement with the biblical text. In this chapter's development, I do not follow a purely biblical study approach but adopt a theological (or ideological) reading. It is also important to note that this study is contextually situated, as I primarily reflect on this issue from my observations in the UK. By acknowledging this project's underlying agenda, I hope readers will profit from reading it and consider the metaphor's implications for their own context.

3. "Global Trends Report," https://www.unhcr.org/global-trends-report-2023, 6. See also "Data Finder." Refugee Data Finder, UNHCR: The UN Refugee Agency, n.d. https://www.unhcr. org/refugee-statistics/download/?url=8qmHH7. To understand the categories on that page see "Who is Included in UNHCR Statistics?" Refugee Data Finder, UNHCR: The UN Refugee Agency, n.d. https://www.unhcr.org/refugee-statistics/methodology/definition/.

4. García, Carmen Aguilar, and Pamela Duncan, "One in Six People Living in England and Wales Born outside UK, Census Reveals." In *The Guardian*, 2 November 2022. https://www. theguardian.com/uk-news/2022/nov/02/one-in-six-people-living-england-wales-were-born-different-country-census-reveals.

tion, and discrimination.[5] Displacement from one's homeland often results in disorientation; immigrants must navigate unfamiliar cultural, social, and political landscapes. The struggle of not belonging is particularly acute for second generation immigrants who often feel disconnected from both their parents' homeland and their new country, somehow living in a liminal space.[6]

In addition to the challenges of displacement and disorientation, immigrants often face discrimination from other people groups within their new society. For instance, British political debates depict immigrants as parasites, leeches, or bloodsuckers; their arrival into the country is often described as a plague, flood, or wave.[7] This language is not only dehumanizing, but it also suggests that immigrants have nothing to offer to the UK, that immigrants are a reality external to the body (the country), and that immigrants are uninvited strangers who deplete life (the country's resources). The terms "plague," "flood," and "wave" also describe their arrival as an unexpected and unavoidable disaster. However, we need to recognize that not everyone in the UK views immigrants in this negative light. The recent refugee crisis in Ukraine witnessed many British people showing remarkable hospitality towards Ukrainian refugees.

Immigration is a challenge for receiving countries which must adjust and provide a welcoming environment while ensuring that their citizens are looked after. But we must emphasize that it is significantly more challenging for those leaving their countries. Although living physically in one place, immigrants live emotionally in two worlds; as a result, they are impacted by what is happening not only in their new country of residence but also in their place of origin. For instance, in London a Ukrainian pastor struggles to unite Russian and Ukrainian church members who used to share fellowship until the war between these countries erupted in February 2022. This conflict has strained their relationship, despite their shared faith. As a result, many church mem-

---

5. For instance, the Nationality and Borders Act 2022 is a UK immigration law that aims to overhaul the UK's immigration system and make it more difficult for asylum seekers to enter the country. This law introduces new measures such as offshore processing centres, increased use of detention, and criminalizing unauthorized entry to the UK. Critics argue that these measures may violate the rights of refugees and asylum seekers, exposing them to further harm and exploitation. As a result, this policy has faced criticism for potentially undermining the UK's obligations under international law, including the 1951 Refugee Convention.

6. Asian-American scholars use the concept of liminality to refer to a transitional or in-between state or space that is neither fully one thing nor the other. The standard rules and boundaries are suspended, ambiguous, and uncertain. See Lee, Sang Hyun. Minneapolis: Fortress Press, 2010.

7. Musolff, Andreas. "Dehumanising Metaphors in UK Immigrant Debates in Press and Online Media," 3, no. 1 (2015): 41–56.

bers are now hesitant to take the Lord's supper together. With these factors at play, unity within the immigrant church[8] emerges as a formidable challenge.

Displacement, disorientation, and discrimination create many emotional, psychological, and financial struggles. In Christian parlance, we refer to these realities as suffering. The prosperity gospel, a popular teaching in some Christian circles, asserts that material wealth and success are signs of God's favour, while suffering and poverty are indicators of a deficient faith or lack of financial commitment.[9] Quite surprisingly, the prosperity gospel's message is appealing to immigrants who are already facing significant challenges – hoping for a quick solution to their suffering, they place their faith in material wealth rather than in Christ.

Of course, not all immigrants have a challenging experience. For many, their arrival in a new country represented the first seeds of hope that began to sprout in fertile soil. Rishi Sunak, the current UK Prime Minister, has ethnic roots elsewhere, and his main challenge is not necessarily displacement or discrimination. Instead, his political obstacle is the vast difference in wealth between himself and the general population, requiring an intelligent approach to bridge the credibility gap.

In *Second City: Birmingham and the Forging of Modern Britain*, Richard Vinen examines the impact of two significant diaspora communities on the city: the Irish and the West Indian. Vinen asserts that these communities shaped Birmingham's identity, contributing to the city's social fabric. Although these people initially arrived in the UK with plans to return home soon, they decided to stay indefinitely in the UK. Various factors contributed to their decision: overcoming considerable challenges, economic opportunities, security, and the hope for a better future.[10]

Immigration has two faces, presenting both challenges and opportunities. Indeed, the process of immigrating is complex and multifaceted, encompassing displacement, disorientation, and discrimination, which affects individuals, families, communities, and churches alike. But, on the flip side, immigration brings cultural diversity, economic growth, and innovation, enriching the lives

---

8. A diaspora church is a religious community composed of individuals and families who have migrated from their country of origin and have settled in a new country, often maintaining cultural ties to their homeland. In this chapter, I will use the terms "immigrant church" and "diaspora church" interchangeably, as both terms point to churches that serve the spiritual needs of immigrants while also providing a sense of community and cultural connection.

9. The prosperity gospel is a complex movement. While more nuanced versions emphasize empowerment rather than abuse, they are rare to find.

10. Vinen, Richard. London: Penguin Books, 2022.

of both newcomers and the host society. Now, we will turn our attention to the past, to the world of 1 Peter, where the audience seems to have experienced only the negative aspects of this reality.

The World of 1 Peter

Hardship was an experience familiar to Peter's first readers. The letter's greeting describes them as a group of early Christian communities living in various parts of Asia Minor (present-day Turkey). Peter addresses "God's elect, exiles scattered throughout the provinces of Pontus, Galatia, Cappadocia, Asia, and Bithynia" (1 Pet 1:1). These early Christian communities were likely composed of both Jewish and gentile converts to Christianity.

The phrase "exiles scattered throughout," as Karen H. Jobes suggests, may refer to a specific geographical context – all five regions the passage mentions were under Roman jurisdiction during Emperor Claudius's reign. If so, the readers were Christians who had been converted elsewhere, perhaps in Rome. They were subsequently uprooted from their homes and relocated against their will to these regions. This displacement contributed to their sense of disorientation, causing them to be exiles in an unfamiliar land.[11]

When used literally, "exile" refers to the state of living away from one's homeland or country of origin due to political, social, or economic reasons. In the metaphorical sense, "exile" refers to the experience of being isolated or excluded from a particular group or community. To properly understand the concept of exile, we must learn *who* was exiled, *where* they were exiled (both to and from), *why* they were exiled, *how long* they have been exiled, and the *consequences* of their exile (the impact it has on them, their families, and their communities).

In 1 Peter, the author sheds light on the believers' severe persecution and suffering. They were being physically harmed or killed for their faith at the hands of the Roman Empire (1 Pet 3:14, 17), and this persecution had caused many of them to fear that the end was near (1 Pet 4:7). In addition to physical suffering, these Christians were being shunned by their families and communities, making it challenging for them to maintain their social and economic wellbeing in a community-oriented culture that placed a high value on honour and shame (1 Pet 4:4). Plus, they were likely struggling with doubts, fears, and the temptation to compromise their faith to avoid persecution (1 Pet 5:6–7).

---

11. Jobes, Karen H. *1 Peter*. BECNT. Grand Rapids: Baker Academic, 2005, esp. 28–41, 63–66.

These passages show that these believers endured severe physical suffering, social ostracism, and internal conflict while navigating life as exiles.

As Peter writes, the suffering and persecution these communities faced were not isolated incidents; their struggles seemed to be part of the persecution of Christians Rome had instigated. In his letter, Peter compares Rome to Babylon (1 Pet 5:13), linking his readers' experience with Israel's exile under Babylon's tyrannic rule. Peter's message is clear: this is not the first time the people of God have encountered intense opposition. Babylon – in the audience's case, Rome – is actively working against God and his people. Hence, Peter stresses that the audience's suffering is part of the larger tapestry: the adversary's predatory work lies behind the empire's evil institutions, attempting to devour the audience's faith (1 Pet 5:8–9). The suffering of these communities, which at first glance may seem like isolated and fragmented pieces, are threads woven into the same fabric.

Recognizing this shared experience of suffering, Peter emphasizes the need for unity and support within the Christian community – he encourages believers to be compassionate and loving towards one another, even when suffering unjustly (1 Pet 3:8–9). Peter stresses the importance of not repaying evil with evil, which could cause disunity. After all, it is one thing to assist others while *they* are suffering; it is another to continue loving others when *we* are suffering too.[12] Maintaining faithfulness while experiencing severe suffering was challenging for the early Christians in Asia Minor – it created a temptation to drift away from the faith. Peter therefore emphasizes the audience's identity, spiritual growth, and ethical living.

In sum, hardship, persecution, and suffering have marked Christian communities worldwide since the beginning. How does Peter reaffirm the exiled believers' identity, promote spiritual growth, and encourage ethical living? How can Peter reaffirm that these exiles are not scattered but are a cohesive entity? If the audience's experience is negative, how can Peter invite them to see their circumstances differently? In what follows, I will reflect on one of the many strategies Peter uses to answer these questions: the use of metaphors. Peter affirms that those in a right relationship with God are God's chosen people.

---

12. The COVID-19 pandemic, an experience still fresh in our memories, reminds us that suffering is disorienting. And even worse, it traps us into making the world revolve around ourselves. Amid the pandemic, did we find motivation to serve in extreme situations of need in Jesus's name? Or do we humbly need to confess that we simply wanted to distance ourselves from the infectious and needy?

Peter's Metaphors: Exile and People Group

After delving into the experience of being an exile, it is essential to understand the concept of belonging to a "people group" for one can only recognize oneself as an exile when uprooted from that place of belonging. To start, it is worth noting that the term "people of God" is, in fact, a metaphor. Of course, this language is so deeply ingrained in our sermons and songs that it is easily overlooked. The logic is the following: first, the recurring use of the term λαός (laós, "people") throughout the New Testament indicates that this descriptor had an established meaning in the early Christian community. For instance, the language "people of God" is used as a reference to Israel (Rom 11:1–2; 15:10; and Heb 11:25) and to the Old Testament promises that announced the inclusion of those who were not originally God's people (2 Cor 6:16; Rom 9:25; Heb 8:10). Second, Peter's letters use the term λαός ("people") to refer to his audience as God's people in 1 Peter 2:9–10 and to describe Israel in 2 Peter 2:1. As such, Peter's use of "people of God" is consistent with what we see in the rest of the New Testament.

Third, the language "people of God" is not used according to the community's everyday use in the first century. In Greco-Roman literature, the term λαός ("people") could refer to a group in general, the mass of a community, or a specific group of people bound together by their shared cultural and historical roots.[13] In alignment with this definition, we could say that Peter's audience understands itself as a collective, a group of people somehow defined by or related to "God." Hence, they are the "people of God." The problem is this: Peter does not just leave them there. He fleshes out what he means, defining and anchoring the concept of "people of God" in Israel's experience in the Old Testament: they are a chosen clan, a holy nation, and royal priests. And this is why, in the text, "people of God" is a metaphor.

Our brief survey above shows that "people of God" refers to a recognized bounded collective (that is, the Israel of God) already defined in the Old Testament. And it is this collective's identity and unique relationship that is figuratively applied to the audience, who would not naturally understand itself as the Israel of God. The transfer of concepts and perspectives from one scenario to another – understanding A in terms of B – is what a metaphor conveys. I would like to suggest that what we have in 1 Peter 2:9–10 is a story metaphor. As David L. Richter explains, in a story metaphor the author's "intended mean-

---

13. Bauer, Walter, and Frederick William Danker. *A Greek–English Lexicon of the New Testament and Other Early Christian Literature*, 3rd ed. Chicago: University of Chicago Press, 1979, s.v. λαός 3.

ing may not be fully understood without activating the story and applying it to the subject of the remark."[14] In a story metaphor, stories are mentioned or alluded to with an expectation that listeners understand the reference and activate their underlying story (e.g. "he's a *prodigal son*"; "she's a *good samaritan*"; "an *exodus* is taking place in Venezuela"). The story that is activated in 1 Peter 2:9–10 is the constitution of God's covenant people in Exodus 19. Thus, when Peter writes, "You are a people for God's possession," he is applying it to a broader group, suggesting that they are not simply absorbed within that group but explained and defined by it.

By viewing themselves through the lens of this metaphor, believers from different ethnic, cultural, and social backgrounds can find common ground and see themselves as a cohesive entity because of their shared spiritual identity as God's chosen people. This collective identity, rooted in the Old Testament story of Israel, transcends the divisions and differences that may otherwise separate them. For the audience, the invitation is to see themselves, their relationship with God, and their circumstances through the lens of this story metaphor.

Having explained why the language "people of God" should be read metaphorically, we need to tap into the logic behind social groups. In the New Testament letters, we learn that the Christian community uses various concepts to describe themselves, including brothers and sisters (ἀδελφοί / *adelphoí*), believers (πιστοί / *pistoí*), saints (ἅγιοι / *hágioi*), the assembly (ἐκκλησία / *ekklesia*), disciples (μαθηταί / *mathētaí*), the way (ὁδός / *hodós*), and Christian (Χριστιανός / *Christianós*).[15] These descriptions are helpful, since they highlight one of the boundaries of the group – whether God's adoption, with "brothers and sisters"; faith, with "believers"; distinct living, with "saints." In our case, "people of God" highlights that the audience is God's possession. Being God's possession means being in the hands of God: God protects them; God claims them; God is responsible for them; God's authority rules them. Being God's people means being constituted around God and God's salvific acts. The members of God's people are those who live in a relationship with God *and* with those who are his own.

---

14. Ritchie, David L. *Metaphorical Stories in Discourse*. Cambridge: Cambridge University Press, 2017, esp. 17.

15. Paul R. Trebilco examines how individuals and groups in the New Testament used self-designations to define their identities and roles. Trebilco argues that self-designations are an essential key to understanding the social and historical context of the New Testament, which were also integral to the author's argument in his letters; see Trebilco, Paul R. *Self-Designations and Group Identity in the New Testament*. Cambridge: Cambridge University Press, 2012.

Peter suggests that the Gentiles were previously excluded from this group because they were not a part of the story of election and covenant that defined the identity of God's people in the Old Testament. What was probably striking, though, was the depiction of the gentiles as "not a people." From the readers' perspective, they could identify with their ethnic group as a people. However, when viewed from the standpoint of God's people – the proper place of belonging – they did not exist as an integrated group endowed with God's privileges, promises, and presence. Hence, the "people of God" has always had a boundary – only those united to God through covenant are *in*. Let us see how Peter threads these essential connections. Peter writes that his audience is "a people for God's possession" (1 Pet 2:10), drawing on the imagery of Exodus 19. In this context, the Israelites find themselves at the foot of Mount Sinai after being miraculously delivered from slavery in Egypt. This event serves as the backdrop for a defining moment in their history: the establishment of the covenant between God and his people. The covenant at Sinai is rooted in God's promise to Abraham, Isaac, and Jacob, demonstrating God's faithfulness in fulfilling those promises.

In Exodus 19:4–6, God reminds the Israelites of their recent deliverance: "You yourselves have seen what I did to Egypt, and how I carried you on eagles' wings and brought you to myself." God then establishes the terms of the covenant, stating that if the Israelites obey his voice and keep his covenant, they will be his treasured possession, a kingdom of priests, and a holy nation. According to Exodus 19:5, when God divided the nations and set boundaries for the peoples, he reserved a portion for himself: the people of Israel. This highlights the special relationship between God and Israel and their unique position as God's chosen people. Peter transfers the value, status, and importance of Israel's relationship with God to his audience's relationship with God through Christ. Through their faith in Christ, the believers who make up the church are also a unique and special possession of God, chosen and set apart for his purposes – by God's initiative.

In 1 Peter 3 and 4, baptism is the embodied practice that represents crossing the boundary line. Baptism transfers individuals from the realm of sin to the realm of Christ, for believers pledge their allegiance to Christ through baptism. Baptism is a public declaration of faith, a way of identifying oneself as a member of the community of God's possession. Peter links baptism to Christ's suffering, emphasizing that just as Christ suffered, those baptized will also suffer. The original audience of this epistle – likely facing persecution and hardships – may have initially interpreted their suffering as a sign of divine disapproval. Hence, Peter shows that Jesus is a "rejected stone" (1 Pet 2:4–8).

Their suffering and rejection are not signs of God's disapproval – even the Saviour, who was without sin, experienced suffering and rejection by the world. Suffering then becomes a mark of belonging rather than a mark of rejection. Linking baptism with suffering underscores the idea that becoming a part of the community of God's possession is not a path to an easy life, but rather a commitment to following in the footsteps of Christ, even in times of suffering. As Peter writes, "For Christ also suffered once for sins, the righteous for the unrighteous, to bring you to God. He was put to death in the body but made alive in the Spirit" (1 Pet 3:18).

Although the institution of the Lord's supper is not explicitly mentioned in 1 Peter, the letter assumes it as a sign of the covenant in the introduction of 1 Peter 1:2: "According to the foreknowledge of God the Father, in the sanctification of the Spirit, for obedience to Jesus Christ and for *sprinkling with his blood*: May grace and peace be multiplied to you." However, a question may emerge: How do covenant, being sprinkled with blood, and the Lord's supper connect? According to Luke, Jesus celebrated the last supper with his disciples and said to them: "This cup is the new covenant in my blood, which is poured out for you" (Luke 22:20). When saying so, Jesus alluded to Exodus 24:8, and both Exodus 19 and Exodus 24 are where the people are constituted and sustained and renewed in their identity as "one people."

The language of "sprinkled blood" Peter uses evokes the text of Exodus 24, where blood, covenant, and eating together are shown to be intimately connected. Exodus 24:6, 9–11 reads as follows.

> Moses took half of the blood and put it in bowls, and the other half he sprinkled on the altar . . . Moses and Aaron, Nadab and Abihu, and the seventy elders of Israel went up and saw the God of Israel. Under his feet was something like a pavement made of lapis lazuli, as bright blue as the sky. But God did not raise his hand against these leaders of the Israelites; they saw God, and they ate and drank.

The significance of this connection lies in the fact that the language of sprinkled blood, which might immediately evoke the idea of sacrifice, actually conveys the idea of covenant. The passage in Exodus 24 reveals the close association between blood, covenant, and eating together, all of which are central elements of the Lord's supper. The covenant established between God and his people is a covenant sealed with the shedding of blood and celebrated with a shared meal. And Peter draws attention to this important concept in the opening words of his letter.

Peter's Solution to his Readers' Suffering and Exile

By stating that they are "a people for God's possession" and "once you were not a people, but now you are his people," Peter evokes a story metaphor in which an event becomes the experience that sheds light on a current situation or individuals. Peter encourages the audience to see themselves as part of the same story of redemption that began with Israel in the Old Testament. It is an invitation for the readers to see themselves in that story, to live by it.

But there is something else going on. Peter uses Exodus 19 to elicit a different response from the audience than the one the Israelites displayed. The Israelites were often disobedient and rebellious, grumbling and complaining in the face of opposition. Peter urges believers to respond to persecution and suffering with faith, love, and perseverance, rather than with complaint and rebellion. But Peter does not only offer the example of Israel; he also encourages his readers to follow the example of Christ, who endured suffering and persecution for the sake of others.

Peter hopes that the audience will hold fast to their faith even during trials, and that is why his use of the metaphor "people of God" occurs in the context of severe suffering. This emphasis contrasts with how this metaphor is used in the rest of the New Testament. In the early Christian church, as the gospel message spread to different regions and cultures, the metaphor "people of God" described the growing community of believers who pledged their allegiance to Jesus as Lord and Saviour. In particular, the metaphor describes the relationship between Jews and gentiles, highlighting that both groups were equal members of God's chosen people. But in 1 Peter, the context is severe hardship.

Hence, the metaphor "people of God" fosters community and unity. By positioning his readers as part of the "people of God," Peter reminds them that they are all part of a larger spiritual gathering. The metaphor "people of God" encourages obedience and faithfulness, reminding readers of their responsibilities as members of God's chosen people. But it also inspires hope and confidence, reminding readers that they are not alone in their struggles and have a supportive community of believers to rely on. The metaphor "people of God" points to the unique purpose and mission that God has for his people: "You are a *people* for God's possession, that you may declare the praises of him who called you out of darkness into his wonderful light" (1 Pet 2:9). This metaphor reminds them of their role in implementing God's will.

Remember that Peter's letter is addressed to a community of believers suffering for their faith. Despite their difficult circumstances, they are called to declare God's praises, which becomes the new horizon the metaphor opens up. Peter encourages his audience to remain faithful and to continue living in a way that reflects their identity as the "people of God." He reminds them that their faithfulness and obedience can be a powerful witness to those around them, especially their unbelieving husbands, neighbours, and masters.

For instance, in 1 Peter 3:1–2, Peter specifically addresses wives who are married to unbelieving husbands, urging them to live in such a way that their husbands may be won over to faith by their conduct. Similarly, in 1 Peter 2:12, Peter encourages his readers to "keep your conduct among the Gentiles honourable, so that when they speak against you as evildoers, they may see your good deeds and glorify God on the day of visitation." In this way, Peter highlights the importance of living out one's faith even amid suffering and hardship by using one's conduct as a powerful testimony about the God to whom we belong.

Whether physically uprooted from their country of origin or living exilically in their own land because of their faith, Peter invites this group of believers to live in hope by understanding themselves as the "people of God." The following poetic lines echo that invitation to readers as they contemplate their own circumstances:

> In foreign lands, I find my place
> A stranger seeking God's embrace.
> My heart, it yearns for love and peace,
> In this new world, where fears increase.
>
> From distant shores and memories past,
> I've come to build a life that lasts.
> My heart, it aches for home and kin,
> Yet in this journey, I've found Him.
>
> A thousand whispers in the air,
> Of unfamiliar tongues, they glare.
> But in this chaos, I find grace,
> As God's own people greet my race.
>
> Now, amidst the struggle and strife,
> His love, it anchors my whole life.
> I stand with brothers, sisters, all,
> Let us obey our Father's call.
>
> No longer lost, alone, or torn,
> In his embrace, I'm safe, reborn.
> United, rise, God's chosen clan,
> From every tribe and tongue, we stand.

Peter's Solution for Christian Immigrants Today

Our experiences as an ethnic people group shape us. If we come from a small and powerless nation, we will likely tend to cooperate and agree to participate in preventative measures. On the contrary, if we come from a privileged group, we will likely attempt to cling to "rights." Either way, if we are to properly model what it means to be God's people, we need to recognize our own presuppositions. We need our minds to be transformed and our narratives recast by Peter's language and its deep connection to Israel's story.

We have established that "people of God" is a metaphor. Metaphors highlight certain aspects while hiding others. Failing to grasp the metaphorical meaning of "people of God" can lead to misleading political readings that obscure the text's essential message. For instance, Peter's language creates a new classification of humanity: those who are in and those who are out. But this language needs to be understood in Peter's address. An inappropriate use of this language can contribute to a sense of superiority, leading to a divisive and contentious mentality toward those outside the community. In 1 Peter, the metaphor highlights God's action on behalf of the audience; God's work made them his special possession. In Peter's letter, the point of this language is to provide assurance, not pride; foster humility, not arrogance; create concern, not indifference. Those outside the community can be further marginalized and even dehumanized if misinterpreted.

But there is more at stake. When reading the passage without recognizing the metaphorical nature of "people of God," there is a risk of reinforcing Christian nationalism and taking the focus away from Christ. This approach would prioritize establishing a political nation and placing political leaders at the forefront, rather than focusing on the greater goal of advancing God's kingdom and doing his will. Preferring a political reading over a metaphorical reading (though Peter's letter *does* highlight the political implications for those who submit to Christ's lordship) suggests an over-realized eschatology, disregarding the unfinished work of the Great Commission: to make disciples of all nations, with each disciple being a member of God's people on equal terms. We are God's people living under his rule in the present. However, we long for that moment when "God's dwelling place is . . . among the people, and he will dwell with them. They will be his people, and God himself will be with them and be their God" (Rev 21:3).

On the contrary, using the language of "people of God" in a harmful or divisive manner can hinder the church's mission to announce the excellency of the One who called us from darkness to light (1 Pet 2:9). The central message of the Christian faith is radical love and compassion. But when the metaphor "people of God" reinforces harmful stereotypes, it creates division and undermines the Christianity it claims to promote. Since this is *not* what the metaphor "people of God" entails, it is essential to briefly summarize what it does. The metaphor implies *identity*. It describes the audience's identity as rooted in their relationship with God, rather than in any external privilege such as ethnicity, culture, or nationality. Peter uses Old Testament language to label a gentile majority church (1 Pet 4:4) as "the people of God." At the same time, he refers to those who come from a gentile background, but are without Christ, as pagans. In light of their new identity, they can see and talk about those outside as *ethnē* ("a people"; 1 Pet 2:12 and 4:3).

The metaphor implies *community*. It describes every community of believers as part of a larger body of Christians connected to one another through their shared faith and identity in Christ. This community is privileged, set apart by God and given a special position in the world. The metaphor implies *covenant*. It describes the nature of the bond believers have with God. Both in the Old and New Testaments, people can be in a relationship with God as his people by being in covenant with him. And the audience has a covenantal relationship with God through Christ. Those united with God in a covenant bond can rest assured in the hope of "an inheritance that can never perish, spoil or fade, kept in heaven for" them. They "are shielded by God's power until the coming of salvation" (1 Pet 1:4–5).

Believers today are God's covenant people and celebrating the Lord's supper is the embodiment and reminder of it. The Lord's supper reveals our understanding of God's people, as we discuss who can be invited. This central sacrament is a social leveller within the church. As Paul explains in 1 Corinthians, the Lord's supper is a time when all believers come together to eat and drink in remembrance of Christ's sacrifice. This act of communal eating breaks down social status and privilege barriers, as all believers come to the table on equal footing, sharing in the same bread and cup.

The Lord's supper reminds us that the grace of God is a gift that is given freely; we have been chosen without regard to merit or status. For instance, socioeconomic "haves" may be okay with being in the same congregation with "have-nots," but they naturally assume they are the group's leaders. Their secular wealth and status invade the church and may perpetuate inequity. This mentality can even be baptized if one thinks wealth always signifies God's blessing. But Christ is an undeserved gift from God, not received based on moral and cultural standards, but based on faith. And the Lord's supper is a visible reminder of that truth.

Taking communion together as a community of believers is vital to maintaining a transformed community rooted in grace. Peter urges his readers to love one another deeply and show hospitality without grumbling (1 Pet 1:22; 4:8–9). He also points to the importance of believers living in harmony with one another, submitting to one another, and serving one another (1 Pet 3:8–9; 5:5–6). These teachings on fellowship and unity are consistent with the spirit of the Lord's supper, which strengthens the common bond and shared identity of believers as the "people of God."

When we partake of the bread and cup together, we are reminded of the sacrifice of Christ and the forgiveness of sins available to all who believe. This act of communal eating helps break down social status and privilege barriers. Unfortunately, in a primarily sermon-centric liturgy that fails to prioritize communion, our ability to internalize the truth of our shared identity as God's people can be hindered. It is noteworthy that the members of the Russian church, for example, can sit under the ministry of God's Word but struggle to partake in communion together. This situation is reminiscent of Paul's confrontation with Peter in Galatians 2. Peter's speech did not match his actions when he withdrew from fellowship with the Gentiles.

Preaching is a form of explicit theology,[16] while communion conveys implicit theology.[17] When we rely solely on sermons to teach about the grace of God, we miss the tangible experience of communion with one another. This can result in a shallow understanding of God's grace, a lack of appreciation for Christ's sacrificial love, and a superficial recognition of our need for the rest of God's people. The importance of both preaching and communion in our worship cannot be overstated, as they work together to deepen our faith and strengthen the bonds that unite us as members of God's people.

Concluding Reflections

I want to conclude this chapter where I began, reflecting on the relevance of the metaphor "people of God" for the exilic church today, with a final reflection on an implication for the church in the West, which is living exilically in its own land. First, the metaphor "people of God" reminds the exilic church of its identity as a community of believers. Their identity as God's people transcends their earthly nationality, ethnicity, and culture. Believers in exile are bound together by their faith in God and their relationship with him. We are members of God's people *first*, and we are members of our earthly people groups *second*. It is a source of hope and comfort for people facing the challenges of migration: discrimination, cultural isolation, and economic hardship. The idea that they are part of a larger community of believers loved and valued by God can provide a sense of security and stability in a world that is often uncertain and hostile.

Of course, for Christians who are immigrants and have achieved financial stability, the metaphor reminds them that their position of power and privilege is not for their own benefit; is instead a means for serving and caring for others. In 1 Peter 4:10–11, the author urges readers to use their gifts and resources to serve one another, "as good stewards of God's varied grace." This includes not only financial resources, but also skills, time, and energy. As members of the "people of God," those who have found success and stability are called to use their

---

16. Explicit theology refers to the formal and structured teachings of the Christian faith, often articulated through sermons, Bible studies, and theological writings. This approach to theology is grounded in the intentional communication of biblical principles and doctrines, aiming to provide explicit and systematic instruction on matters of faith, morality, and practice.

17. Implicit theology encompasses the beliefs, values, and ideas communicated through a faith community's practices, rituals, and experiences. This form of theology is less focused on systematic instruction and more on the lived experience of faith. Implicit theology is conveyed through elements such as worship, prayer, fellowship, and the sacraments, which offer tangible and experiential ways of engaging with God and one another.

blessings to bless others and further God's kingdom. Regardless of our status, we are called to serve and work together as God's people under Christ's banner.

Second, the metaphor "people of God" reminds us of Israel's exile. The Jews were instrumental in fulfilling God's purpose, not despite being in exile but because of it. The Jews who went into exile were the stepping stones for establishing the church in the book of Acts, because the exile created the need for the establishment of synagogues, and Paul's strategy was to go to the synagogue (if there was one) whenever he arrived in a city (Acts 9:20; 13:14–16; 17:1–2; 18:4–5). It was because of the Jews in exile that the Old Testament was translated into Greek in Alexandria, and many gentile Christians became familiar with the history of God and his people a few centuries later. As immigrants, God can use us creatively and unexpectedly to enrich the host culture and expand Christ's message.

Third, the metaphor "people of God" can help second generation immigrants navigate the complexities of living between two cultures and two worlds, as they try to balance the expectations of their parents' culture with the norms of the wider society. The metaphor "people of God" can provide a framework for understanding their place in the world and help them to find a sense of belonging that transcends cultural differences.

Fourth, the metaphor "people of God" can provide a sense of purpose and direction in life. As second generation immigrants navigate the challenges of growing up in a foreign land, they may struggle to find meaning and purpose. Being part of a community working towards a common goal gives a sense of direction and focus – a sense of purpose beyond individual goals and aspirations.

Fifth and finally, the metaphor "people of God" reminds the church of its ultimate destination, as it is a foretaste of the final renewal of all things when God will establish his kingdom and his people on earth as it is in heaven. Believers today are already participating in the future reality, ahead of time. And yet, as John writes, "Look! God's dwelling place is now among the people, and he will dwell with them. They will be his people, and God himself will be with them and be their God" (Rev 21:3). The scattered community's current struggles and challenges are temporary. God's people are part of a larger story of God's plan to restore all things. Understanding our identity and belonging as the people of God provides us with a perspective that sustains us through difficult times and inspires us to live with hope and purpose.

The metaphor "people of God" is especially relevant in a Western context, where Christians may face increasing hostility and persecution for their faith. We are called to be conscious of our witness as we navigate a world often at odds with our Christian values and beliefs. In 1 Peter 2:12, Peter urges his readers to "keep your conduct among the Gentiles honourable, so that when they speak against you as evildoers, they may see your good deeds and glorify God on the day of visitation." Peter highlights the importance of living out one's faith as a witness to those who may be sceptical or hostile towards the Christian message. Rather than responding to attacks or hostility similarly, we are called to embody the values and character of the "people of God" in a way that may draw others to faith.

This reading of the "people of God" prevents us from falling into the traps of nationalism, of idolizing our own country or a culture that often prioritizes individualism, consumerism, and self-interest. The political reading of the people of God was used historically in the context of Christian mission and colonization, by some, as a way to justify European subjugation and domination in Africa, Asia, and the Americas. A political reading imposes Western values and practices, destroying indigenous cultures, and exploiting natural resources and labour. Alternatively, a metaphorical reading invites us to collaborate with indigenous peoples, learning from and respecting their cultures as equal members of God's people.

Instead of thinking of ourselves as members of our countries *first* and God's people *second*, we can embrace our identity as the people of God, acknowledging that our allegiance is ultimately to Christ and his agenda. This can help us to resist the temptation to conform to the values of secular culture. As God's people, we have a narrative to live in and to live by.[18] As God's people, we have a narrative for life.

---

18. Although the metaphor "people of God" informs the audience then and now of their reality in God, it only serves as a prism. It provides us with a facet of a more extensive understanding of our identity and mission here. Other images used in the New Testament, explored throughout the rest of this book, would reinforce, enhance, and contribute to a more comprehensive understanding and experience of the church's identity and mission.

6

Light: The Guiding Force of God's Kingdom

Sergiy Tymchenko

You are the light of the world. A town built on a hill cannot be hidden. Neither do people light a lamp and put it under a bowl. Instead they put it on its stand, and it gives light to everyone in the house. In the same way, let your light shine before others, that they may see your good deeds and glorify your Father in heaven. (Matt 5:14–16, NIV[1])

Introduction

In late October 2022, I was driving east with two other volunteers who had been pastors and my friends for many years. Our destination was Kovsharivka, a town with a few blocks of large nine-story apartment buildings a few kilometres from the front line where Ukrainian forces were resisting Russian invaders. Kovsharivka had recently been liberated by the Ukrainian army, and at the time was a completely unfunctional township. A local factory, the place of work for most of Kovsharivka's ten thousand residents, was destroyed. The settlement looked as if there were no life in it. It was completely quiet and empty. The Ukrainian army had moved on, pushing the Russian occupiers eastward, and people hid in their cold, dark apartments, waiting for someone to come and turn their social life back on. After a while, one by one, people

---

1. All Scripture quotations in this chapter are taken from the NIV.

started coming out of their homes. They saw the inscription "Volunteers" on our two large vans and realized that we had brought them food. There were very few smiles on their faces, but they seemed grateful for the packages of food and some hygiene items. The sober atmosphere suddenly changed when they realized that, in addition to the food, they also received two large candles for each family. We saw their faces brighten and they began to talk, thanking us for the candles. I still remember two boys, ten or twelve years old, hugging their candles and smiling the happiest smiles I can remember in my life. They seemed to realize that their long nights would no longer be so dark, scary, and gloomy. The candles meant for them not only light, but also play, communication, laughter – the things we adults call "social life."

The light metaphor of Jesus is fascinating. It is both simple to understand and rich in applications. It reaches us immediately through our own experiences and stories we have heard from others. It connects us with special memories of those who have enlightened our lives emotionally, cognitively, or spiritually.

Let me say a few words about myself. I have lived almost all my life in Ukraine, grew up in a Christian family, and later became a pastor and seminary lecturer. I have been both a witness and a participant in the history of the evangelical church in Ukraine since the 1960s. I remember the time of persecution of the church, when believers gathered for secret services during the communist regime; the time of the church's dizzying growth after the collapse of the Soviet Union; more recently, when the first volunteer evangelical chaplains went to the front lines to support soldiers in their unequal struggle against a powerful, aggressive empire; and now, when believers are looking for ways to serve and support their country as it tries to withstand a potentially fatal attack from Russia. Throughout my life, I have seen that Christians in Ukraine have always reflected the light of Christ, although it has not at all times reached people with the same intensity and brightness. Looking back, I now have a deeper understanding from which to discuss Jesus's metaphor of light in the context of Ukraine's recent history.

Mission of Light

It was January 1989. I was on my way to a meeting with four other young Baptist pastors in Tallinn, the capital of what was then Soviet Estonia. A high-ranking Estonian lawyer, who was a new believer at the time, agreed to help us write an official letter to the Moscow Kremlin, asking them to allow us to register a Christian mission to preach the gospel throughout the Soviet Union. It was a risky move; no one knew in 1989 where *perestroika*, the newly proclaimed course of social restructuring, would lead the atheistic Soviet empire. Our new Estonian friend was going to help us not only with writing the request, but also with submitting it to the central government in Moscow.

Before writing the request for registration, there was one urgent issue that needed to be resolved: our mission still had no name. All five of us knew that we had to agree on a name for our mission before we met with the lawyer. As I sat by the window, I tried to find a name in the Bible that would best fit our bold initiative. The plane was approaching Tallinn, but my search for a good biblical name was still ongoing. At one point my work was interrupted as the plane entered a zone of dark grey clouds and the cabin lights were turned off. Suddenly, I was blinded by a bright beam of light. It came through the window from the sun, which broke through a gap in the clouds, through the reflection of my Bible, which was open to the Gospel of John. In the next second, I had no doubt that the name for our mission would be *The Light of the Gospel*. Half an hour later I saw my friends at the entrance to the Tallinn airport and told them: I know what our mission will be called! Everyone smiled. They loved the name.

In 1990, we acquired registration. By 1995, Light of the Gospel missionaries had planted more than 250 new churches, often in the most remote areas of the (by then) former Soviet Union. Many of these churches were called "Light of the Gospel." Apparently, the metaphorical meaning of this name sounded attractive to many people who had never even read the Bible before. Many of those who lived all their life behind the Iron Curtain told me at that time how deeply they were shocked by *glasnost* ("openness") – the new freedom to have uncensored access to information. They now realized the depth of the former regime's moral darkness and were looking for new meaning in their lives. The gospel message offered them some hope – a new light in life. Those who were becoming believers knew – their lives had been changed by the light of the gospel.

Metaphor of Light

The effectiveness of metaphors in general, and biblical metaphors in particular, is often based on their ability to surprise listeners with an unexpected comparison and to engage them in exploring new aspects of a subject. This is exactly what Jesus did when he called his disciples "the light." He surprised them by ascribing to them a trait of his own identity, the light that the Old Testament prophets had pointed to in describing the future coming of the Messiah (Isa 9:2; 30:26; 49:6; Zech 14:6, cf. John 8:12; 9:5). He also invited them to reflect on the magnitude of the task he had entrusted to them – to deal with the problem of darkness in the world.

The light metaphor is one of the first two metaphors (together with the metaphor of salt) used by Jesus to describe the features that distinguish his disciples from other people in the world: "You are the light of the world. . . . let your light shine before others" (Matt 5:14, 16). Distinct qualities of the light and salt make them invaluable and irreplaceable in the world.[2]

From the immediate context, we see that it is the connection with Jesus and conformity to the humble qualities of those who inherit his kingdom (Matt 5:5–12) that gives his disciples an ability to penetrate the world with a positive effect. They can do it either as salt, protecting it from moral decay, or as light – pointing to the reality hidden by the moral darkness of deception and corruption. The connection with the source and the distinction from the environment is important in both cases. Something that looks like salt has a salt value only when it has connection with the real salt. A city built on a hill cannot be overlooked because of the hill on which it stands. A lamp being lit and freed from a cover makes a distinct difference in the dark room (5:13–16). These explanations of the metaphor should make us humble: we are not useful because of our personal qualities, it is not about us, but about our connection.

Throughout this chapter we will explore two requirements for the church underlined by this metaphor. The first is to be distinct from the world and the second is to be connected to Jesus. As we will see, these two requirements are necessary for the church to maintain its true identity and fulfil its mission of reflecting and spreading Christ's light in the world. It is impossible to contem-

---

2. Klein, William W. *Become What You Are: Spiritual Formation According to the Sermon on the Mount.* Downers Grove: Biblica Books, 2006, esp. 78.

plate light without considering darkness. By giving two examples of how the church shall be the light of the world, Jesus points to the general problems its light will address and correct. A town built on a hill provides orientation. A lamp that is lit spreads light, showing the community what is real and what is dangerous (5:13–16). An oppositional metaphor of darkness is paired with the metaphor of light and describes social problems of disorientation, confusion, deception, and hidden evil. To appreciate the scope and seriousness of the world's darkness problem we only need to look at the latest news online. To understand its meaning and roots we need to consider the broad biblical context which was familiar to the first readers of the gospel.

The metaphor of light used by Jesus immediately reminds us of some key images from the Bible. Indeed, the very first words of God recorded in the Hebrew Scriptures were "Let there be light." In this liturgical Hebrew song written on the first page of the Bible, the creation of light and separating it from the darkness was instrumental for the beginning of God's creation process (Gen 1:1–5). It is hard to miss that day and night created by God in his first "day" during the first three days of creation were not governed by the "two great lights" – the sun and the moon (1:14–19). Instead, they were simply called: "light" and "darkness" (1:3–5). John Walton argued that Genesis 1:3–5 describes creation of the "time" system where "day" and "night" have not a material sense, but a *functional* one. Initiating light in the midst of darkness was about bringing order and the possibility of life in the world that knew only chaos before God's act of creation.[3] In fact, all God's creation activity as described in Genesis 1 is about bringing the world from formlessness and chaos to structure and order. "The surface of the deep" (1:2), as Walton explains, is "primeval cosmic waters [which] are the classic form that nonexistence takes in the functionally oriented ancient world."[4]

To better appreciate how Walton's analysis of the creation story may help our understanding of the light metaphor given by Jesus, let's take a look on the remake of the Genesis 1 song written in the beginning of John 1.[5] We read that in the beginning "all things were made through him" (i.e., through Jesus; v. 3), and that now he, the Word incarnate, continues to give new life to the perishing world. The light metaphor in this poem shows the availability of God's power to change the lives of people by sharing his eternal life with everyone: "In him

---

3. Walton, John. *The Lost World of Genesis One: Ancient Cosmology and the Origins Debate.* Downers Grove: IVP Academic, 2009, esp. 56.

4. Walton, *The Lost World of Genesis One*, 48.

5. The prologue to the Gospel of John was probably an ancient Christian hymn.

was life, and that life was the light of all mankind" (John 1:4). Like the light of the sun renews the life of plants in the morning, the light of Jesus gives new life to humans, reaching them in their dark places (1:5, 9). "In the beginning," Jesus's power to create light brought the world into existence out of the darkness of chaos; today it means bringing new meaning to people's lives, restoring them from the darkness of sin that paralyzes their existence (John 1:5, 9). They can accept the light, receiving new life from God, or reject this offer (1:11, 12).

Another key image of light in the Bible is associated with the glory of God revealed in his visible presence with the people of Israel, covered by bright light in a cloud or in fire. This phenomenon reminded people that God is the highest reality in the world, the most powerful, just, and valuable reality they could imagine.[6] The seraphim in Isaiah's vision expanded this image of God's visible presence when they announced that "the whole earth is full of his glory" (Isa 6:3), a reflection of his superlative holiness. This holiness describes God's character as it becomes clear from the response of the prophet (Isa 6:5) and, as John N. Oswalt rightly notes, from the description of the holy character of God in Leviticus 18–25.[7] Later we read in the book of Isaiah that nations will be attracted by the reality (glory) of God's character when they see its reflection through the people of God.

> Arise, shine, for your light has come,
>   and the glory of the LORD rises upon you.
> See, darkness covers the earth
>   and thick darkness is over the peoples,
> but the LORD rises upon you
>   and his glory appears over you.
> Nations will come to your light,
>   and kings to the brightness of your dawn.
> (Isa 60:1–3)

It is within the framework of this metaphor that we read twice in the Gospel of John the words of Jesus: "I am the light of the world" (8:12; 9:5). The one who is himself the agent of creation (1:3), the Logos and the eternal "I am" (4:26) does not give his followers halos around their faces to impress people, but the ability to reflect God's character even when they themselves do not

---

6. Exodus 25:8; 29:45, cf. 40:34–35; 1 Kings 8:11; Isaiah 60:1–3. This phenomenon was described by the word for glory, "*kabod*" in Hebrew, which had the root idea of heaviness, weightiness, or worthiness. In post-biblical Judaism it was described by the term "*shekhinah*," the "radiance."

7. Oswalt, John N. *Isaiah*. NIV Application Commentary 5. Grand Rapids: Zondervan, 2003, esp. 646.

have the most attractive appearance. The true holiness of God is able to heal and restore life out of chaos and show the way to order the social life of nations.

Coming together, disciples of Jesus will form distinct communities of light as unmissable for the world as a town built on a hill. Being closely connected with Jesus like a lamp that is lit by its owner, they need to be placed in such a way that everyone could see what is good and what is real. To deal with its darkness and restore functionality the world needs the church that maintains its distinct kingdom of heaven identity and keeps close connection with the Light.

Theology of Light

There are periods in history that we call dark times. In such times, we feel that darkness is taking over entire countries, continents, or the entire world. This often happens when a society is going through some difficulties, and often follows messianic claims by popular leaders who promise their followers salvation from economic, political, and cultural woes. These political messiahs promise a better life, justice, and order. In return, they want to be praised and obeyed; they behave as if they are above the law. They pose as the light of the world but lead the world into darkness. A new order may come, and life may become better for the closest followers of these popular leaders, but only for a while and at a high cost to the whole society. The order typically turns into totalitarian ideological control; a better life for some means loss of justice, suffering, and even death for many and, as a result, the temporary "salvation" from social ills brings increasing dysfunctionality to society. We know about such dark times from the pages of the Bible, as well as from recent history. We can be sure that any political leader who demands unquestioning allegiance and claims a quasi-divine status or divine authorization behaves in the spirit of Antichrist who denies the authority of the Father and the Son.[8]

A theology of light is especially needed in dark times. Isaiah spoke of the hope of God's light for those who lived in the darkness of the Babylonian empire. The Apostle John wrote about the darkness of evil and the light of the Lord in the dark times of imperial worship in the Roman Empire. More recently, Karl Barth (1886–1968) worked on a theology of light, reflecting on the dark times of fascism in Europe. In the turbulent years of World War I and following revolutions, Barth, then a young Swiss pastor, was concerned about the place of followers of Jesus in society. He discussed the church's ability to "penetrate life's hidden corners, and steadily refuse to treat anything – however

---

8. 1 John 2:18, 22; 2 Thessalonians 2:3–11.

trivial or disgusting it may seem – as irrelevant."[9] He wrote that the goal of the church was to demonstrate God's goodness and serve as "parables" or "tokens" of the goodness which, alone, belongs to God.[10] In that context he delivered his lecture, "The Christian in Society," in Germany.[11]

In 1921 Barth moved with his family to Germany where they spent the next fourteen years teaching theology. It was the time after Germany was defeated in the war and signed the very unpopular and controversial Treaty of Versailles. Social problems in Germany were rapidly growing, along with spreading conspiracy theories, radicalization of right political groups, hyperinflation followed by the worldwide depression, business failures, mass unemployment, fear of communism and, finally, in 1933, the coming of Hitler to power. It was during this time that Hitler abolished all democratic processes and initiated the systematic terrorizing of Jews. It was also the time when many leaders of the German Protestant Church Confederation decided to support Hitler's regime and created a movement of "German Christians" aligned with the ideological principles of Nazism. The grip of darkness was becoming increasingly tighter both for society and for the church.

In 1934 Barth became a primary draftsman of the "Barmen Declaration" which exposed the teaching of "German Christians" as false Christianity. In this document, he and other leaders of the Confessing Church declared: "We may not keep silent, since we believe that we have been given a common message to utter in a time of common need and temptation."[12] The Declaration affirmed that God has appointed to the state "the task of providing for justice and peace" and that this task "calls to mind the kingdom of God, God's commandment, and righteousness" and therefore reminds the true community of Christ followers of "the responsibility of both of rulers and of the ruled," calling them to trust and obey the word of God.[13] It also called for opposition to the belief that the state "could become the single and totalitarian order of human life, thus fulfilling the church's vocation as well."[14]

9. Barth, Karl. *The Epistle to the Romans*, translated by E.C. Hoskyns. Oxford: Oxford University Press, 1968 (1933), esp. 425.

10. Barth, *The Epistle to the Romans*, 431 and 436.

11. Karl Barth, "The Christian in Society," in *The Word of God and Theology*, translated by Amy Marga, 31–70. New York: T&T Clark, 2011.

12. "Theological Declaration of Barmen," 8.08, quoted in Arthur C. Cochrane, *The Church's Confession Under Hitler.* Philadelphia: Westminster Press, 1962, 237–242, quotation from p. 237.

13. "Theological Declaration of Barmen," 8.22.

14. "Theological Declaration of Barmen," 8.27.

A few years later, back in Switzerland, Barth reflected on Jesus's light metaphor in his essay *Church and State*: "The light which falls from the heavenly *polis* upon the earthly *ecclesia* is reflected in the light which illuminates the earthly *polis* from the earthly ecclesia, through their mutual relation."[15] Barth's image was clear: the church, the earthly ecclesia, has mutual relations with both heavenly and earthly polices; this is why it can translate the light from heaven to earthly society which is completely blind to heavenly light. The "state" (earthly polis) is blind to the light from the heavenly polis. It was the task of Christ's followers to keep their mutual relations with Christ. By changing their focus and becoming "German Christians," they lost their ability to reflect the light and German society was easily deceived and began to worship Hitler. It was the Confessing Church in Germany that valued its mutual relations with the heavenly polis – God's kingdom. It helped them to oppose social nationalism and risk their lives to call everyone "to mind the kingdom of God, God's commandment, and righteousness."

After World War II, Barth revisited the issue of the mission of the church to the earthly society in his essay, "The Christian Community and the Civil Community."[16] Borrowing and developing the idea partly from Oscar Cullmann, Barth described relations between the church and society as two concentrical circles around the inner centre of the kingdom of Christ. In the figure here, the church is the mediator of the light of Christ and his kingdom to the

---

15. Karl Barth, *Church and State*, translated by G. R. Howe (London: Student Christian Movement Press, 1939), 61; italics emphasis of terms transliterated from Greek original to Barth; *polis* means "city" and *ecclesia* means "asssembly" or "church"; this book was first published in German as *Rechtfertigung und Recht* ("Justification and Justice"; *Recht* can also be translated as "Law").

16. Karl Barth, "The Christian Community and the Civil Community," in *Community, State, and Church: Three Essays*, 149–190, with a new Introduction by David Haddorff (Eugene: Wipf & Stock, 2004); previously published by Anchor Books, 1960.

world and is located between the outer circle – the state or the civil community and the inner circle – the kingdom of God.[17]

The diagram provides some important insights into the biblical perspective of the relations between the two communities. First, the concentric circles convey the idea of likeness as well as the connection between people and their Creator. It reminds us that the world is created by the Grand Designer who made human society in the image of his own being and kingdom. Second, it demonstrates the dual nature of the church which has important connections with both God's kingdom and the earthly, temporal society of sinners. Third, it helps us to see and understand the mission of the church as a light-bearer from the source of light in the centre of the diagram to the society in the Earth, including its most distant "ends." Cullmann's simple imagery indeed helped Barth to develop his analysis of the relations between the two communities and to discuss their practical applications.

Barth's main attention in this essay was focused on the church and its mission to the world. To determine this mission, he needed to specify what the church has that the world does not, showing in what ways the two communities are different from each other. Barth often used the terms "the church" and "the state" interchangeably with the terms "the Christian community" and "the civil community." Talking about the state, he was concerned mostly not with its structure "but with human beings gathered together in corporate bodies to serve the common tasks."[18] As a corporate body of people, the state is different from the church not so much by its institutions and offices, but by its tasks. At the same time, these two communities differ from each other by their allegiances and identities. The state is represented and ruled by the head of its governing institution while the church belongs to the kingdom of God and submits to the rule of its representative – Jesus Christ. The church is impacted by Christ and his kingdom (from the inner circle) and this determines its character and identity. The mission of the church is, in fact, founded on its allegiance to God: "The Christian community is not an end in itself. It serves God and it thereby serves man."[19]

The mission of the church to the state makes sense if it understands itself as a Christian community within a particular civil community. Thus, Christians

---

17. Barth, "The Christian Community and the Civil Community," 155; citing O. Cullman, *Königsherrschaft Christi und Kirche im Neuen Testament* ("Kingship of Christ in the Church and the New Testament"), 1941.

18. Barth, "The Christian Community and the Civil Community," 149.

19. Barth, "The Christian Community and the Civil Community," 166.

in Germany during World War II bore a special responsibility for their German society, although few of them realized their responsibility to bring the light of the gospel to the state. To recognize its mission to the civil community and to keep this mission in focus, the church must understand both what it has in common with the state and to what extent they are different.

The graphically expressed "common centre" of the two communities is an illustration of biblical teaching that they both have some correspondence, a common source, and a similar logic of their existence.[20] Ultimately, the state and the church are different "constants" or "instruments" of the same divine Providence and therefore share a common origin and common centre.[21] According to Barth, the existence of the state can be viewed as an allegory and an analogue to the kingdom of God.[22] The state, he argues, has its just, righteous purposes established by God focused on providing "an external, relative, and provisional order of law"[23] so that "all political questions and all political efforts as such are founded on the gracious ordinance of God by which man is preserved and his sin and crime confined."[24] However, the state has neither the strength nor the will to meet its true criteria, nor even the memory of them. It is the church with its being in the inner circle which is close to the kingdom of God and having knowledge of it through its "mystery of . . . faith and gospel," that can help the state to fulfil its purposes.[25] To fulfil this mission to the civil community, the church needs to be engaged in "the activity that revolves directly around . . . [their] common centre" and at the same time should be "a reflection . . . [and] the content of its own faith and gospel."[26]

To what extent can the state be affected by the church's mission? Shall the church expect that its activity, done correctly, will turn the civil community into the Christian community? In other words, could the line between the two concentric outer circles on the Barth's image of inner and outer circles be blurred? Looking into the Bible, Barth finds that "The Divine purpose is not at all . . . that the state should itself gradually develop more or less into a Church."[27] The identities of both communities will continue to stay unchanged

---

20. Barth, "The Christian Community and the Civil Community," 153–160.
21. Barth, "The Christian Community and the Civil Community," 156.
22. Barth, "The Christian Community and the Civil Community," 169.
23. Barth, "The Christian Community and the Civil Community," 154.
24. Barth, "The Christian Community and the Civil Community," 164.
25. Barth, "The Christian Community and the Civil Community," 169.
26. Barth, "The Christian Community and the Civil Community," 170.
27. Barth, "The Christian Community and the Civil Community," 166.

during the intermediate period between Christ's coming to Earth. It is the structures of the two communities that can attain stronger resemblance to the kingdom of God if the church remembers "represent the inner within the outer circle."[28] To fulfil its mission the church must not make the state "as far as possible subservient to the tasks of the Church."[29] Instead, it should shape its own life by "gather[ing] as it is directly and consciously around the common centre."[30] By doing so, the church does not claim to be the image of the kingdom of God, but, being filled with its light, becomes "the model and prototype of the real state."[31]

To sum up Barth's theology of the church's mission to the state – his understanding of the metaphor of light given by Jesus to his disciples – we may use a figure. The church belongs to the horizontal dimension: secular (civil) society, but it is also connected to and identified with the vertical dimension: the kingdom of God. The first is temporal, the second is eternal.[32]

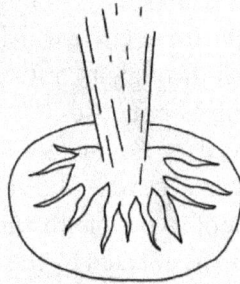

The mission of the church is to give to the temporal society the knowledge of its original design by pointing to the Designer and his eternal kingdom as well as by giving an example of life that takes the kingdom design as its highest goal and standard. The purpose of the state is to provide provisional and relative (temporal) order. It cannot become the church or receive the identity of the kingdom of God. At the same time, the church also shall not pursue

28. Barth, "The Christian Community and the Civil Community," 186.

29. Barth, "The Christian Community and the Civil Community," 166.

30. Barth, "The Christian Community and the Civil Community," 186.

31. Barth, "The Christian Community and the Civil Community," 168, 186.

32. *Saeculum* (Latin): literally "generation, temporal" but used in Ecclesial Latin to mean "the world" as opposed to the Church.

the power given to the state for fulfilling its task. It also shall not expect to be served by the state except by providing conditions where the church can freely preach the gospel.

Positive change in civil society comes with "light" from the kingdom of God through Christ's people who live in society as "agents of light." But this light-identity of Christians, which makes the church a powerful model, only works when they tap into the unlimited energy of the "central circle" by being intimately connected to Jesus Christ through his Spirit. Toward the end of his essay, Barth challenges us, just as he challenged Christians in Germany before the outbreak of World War II: "How can a reformation of the whole people be brought about if it is common knowledge that the Church itself is bent only on self-preservation and restoration – or not even that?"[33] And how, we would add, can the church come to the point of becoming almost invisible in the surrounding secular society, or, even worse, spreading darkness instead of light in a world where a just order is so needed?

Considering Barth's imagery we could notice that its construction suggests possibility of two gaps that make the church less effective or completely ineffective: (1) when there is a distance between the church and the world (separate life) and (2) when there is a distance between the church and God (worldliness).

Light Switch: Separation vs. Engagement

One of my earliest memories from my childhood is my parents singing Christian hymns together, with my father accompanying on guitar. I remember one day I asked my mother to teach me a song. The very first song I learned from her started with these four lines:

> My home in Heaven beyond the clouds here,
> Is where new life starts – eternal days;
> There friends and fam'ly will gather with us
> To sing the Father our songs of praise.[34]

That year I was put in a daycare centre and decided to share the "My Home in Heaven" song with other children and some childcare workers. The next day the director of that centre told my parents that if their child continues such antisocial behaviour in their Soviet institution, they could be denied

---

33. Barth, "The Christian Community and the Civil Community," 186.

34. The translation is taken from https://speakingofthings.blogspot.com/2019/12/my-home-in-heaven.html, accessed 31 January 2024. Later I learned that this song was written in the Gulag by a Christian who was persecuted for his faith during Stalin's regime.

their parental rights. That evening my mom and dad told me that I can sing Christian songs only at home. I remember the question that bothered me after that: "How then will these people know about heaven?"

At that time, in the late 1950s–early 1960s, the Soviet society was immensely proud and enthusiastic about its achievements, especially after being the first country to have "conquered space" by sending up the first *Sputnik* and later the first human, Yuri Gagarin. The Soviet ideology was all about building a perfect society "by themselves" – meaning without God. Nikita Khrushchev, the First Secretary of the Communist Party of the Soviet Union, promised at that time: "The current generation of Soviet people will live under communism."[35] According to the Communist Party's propaganda, religion was a tool used by the capitalist countries to prevent the Soviet people building their perfect society. At that time a new large scale anti-religious campaign in the Soviet Union was undertaken. The church in the USSR was to be kept under more strict control and stronger isolation from the "Soviet society" (literally, and ironically, from the "society of harmony"). Many believers who did not agree to keep their faith secret were persecuted. Thousands of churches were closed and went into "underground" existence.

How could the church be the light of the world when it was forced to live a secret Christian life? There is a hint in the context of Jesus's metaphor of light in the Sermon on the Mount. Just before using the metaphors of salt and light Jesus said his followers must expect persecution "because of righteousness," and that in persecution Christians' light is seen by people when they recognize that what Christians do is "good" (Matt 5:16). The way that Christians behave will give people a chance to start discovering God. In fact, there were quite a few people who noticed the light of God's kingdom that was quietly spreading through believers in the Soviet Union. Some of them were open to talk about God. When, by the end of 1970s, the antireligious campaign slowed down, many new people joined the church. It seemed that the powerful atheist state, despite all its efforts to separate the church from the society behind the Iron Curtain, was unable to turn off the light that Jesus spoke about in his Sermon on the Mount.

In the 1990s during Gorbachev's *perestroika* and *glasnost* in the Soviet Union, the state-imposed gap between the church and society began to fade away. This was the time when the light switch began to turn to the "engagement" position. The Light of the Gospel mission (that was briefly introduced

---

35. Tompson, William J. *Khrushchev: A Political Life*. New York: St. Martin's Press, 1997, esp. 238.

in the beginning of this chapter) was formed at that time as well as hundreds of other missions established over the next few years. But there were some other gaps that the church needed to deal with to reach society.

The ideological gap between the church and post-Soviet society during the first years of freedom was not the main challenge for these new Christian missionaries. The emptiness of the communist ideology was self-evident for many people in the new countries that formed after the collapse of the Soviet Union in 1991. A bigger problem was the cultural gap. During the years when the church was existing in survival mode, it developed an attitude of intolerance to many things in the contemporary secular culture. The range of cultural differences varied between church groups often centred on attitudes toward "modern" trends in fashion, music, and entertainment. As soon as the newly formed evangelical missionary groups realized the need to bridge the cultural gap, their new churches were filled with people from different professions and backgrounds who were eager to serve God with their skills and talents. Older Evangelical churches followed suit one by one, leaving culturally separate churches in the minority.

During more than thirty years of independence, there have been virtually no restrictions on religious freedom in Ukraine. The number of new congregations grew rapidly, especially in the first fifteen years. Newly formed nondenominational Christian professional and student groups were active not only in Ukraine, but also helped to establish similar fellowships in other countries of the former Soviet Union. However, the political life of Ukraine was formed mostly by several business groups and politicians who were oscillating between the political establishment in Russia and opportunities to develop ties with the European Union and its economic market. The illegal benefits from the transportation of Russian gas through Ukrainian territory were shared by dishonest political players in both the East and the West.

The presidential elections of 2004 presented an opportunity for Ukrainian society to get rid of corrupt politicians and powerful oligarchs with criminal ties. But when people realized the elections had been rigged, as the officially announced results clearly contradicted the results of the polls, they took to the central squares of many large cities. On 23 November, the second day of protests, several hundred thousand protesters filled the Maidan, the central square in Kyiv.

That day I was walking among the fast-growing number of tents that protesters were putting up in Khreshchatyk, the central street connected with Maidan. Suddenly, a van stopped near us. A few young believers went out, amazed: they had been praying for a pastor who would stay among the protesters! They unloaded two big tents, erected them right in the middle of the street, and raised two big posters above the tents: "A Prayer Tent" and "Christians stand for truth." Within a few hours we were surrounded by many hundreds of other tents. People were coming from all regions of Ukraine. During the next few days many other pastors and believers joined us near our Maidan Prayer Center. People were bringing their prayer requests 24/7 during the next seventeen days of mass protest.

During the night there were volunteer sentries stationed ten metres apart from each other, guarding the whole street camp and allowing many thousands of people to take their night rest. During one of those nights, I was inside the prayer tent when I heard a muffled conversation between the two guards near me. Suddenly, one of them used a swear word. After a short pause the other man replied: "Shame on you! Don't you understand that this is a holy ground?" What he meant was clear: "there is no place for profanity when people are ready to sacrifice their lives for justice." Later, thinking about the circular diagram above, I often remembered this episode. There is a presence of holiness or kingdom light in the midst of secular society when it struggles for justice and the church supports it in this struggle.

Justice prevailed in Ukraine in 2004; the inauguration of a new president who did not have connections with corrupt oligarchs looked very promising to a majority of Ukrainians. Yet the struggle of Ukraine to become economically independent was doomed to fail without significant help from the West. By 2013, Vladimir Putin felt that he could put the current Ukrainian government under his full control, just as he already controlled Russia. The Kremlin increased its economic and political pressure in its attempt to bring Ukraine under its control. The result was Euromaidan (also called the "Revolution of Dignity") – another national protest during the winter of 2013–2014 that radically changed the political course of Ukraine, led to the Russian annexation of Crimea, and later to the full-scale war with Russia. This time Prayer Tents spontaneously were erected not only in Kyiv's Maidan, but also in the central squares of many cities, most noticeably in Donetsk. Many Christians felt that it was their chance to be with people when they are ready to pay a high price for defending justice and truth.

The Revolution of Dignity ended only when the president and the government fled from the country following the tragic death of more than one hundred protesters who were shot by riot-police snipers. The new chairman of the Parliament became the interim president – he was a known Baptist preacher, Oleksandr Turchynov. At that point, the light switch had been firmly turned to the "engagement" position for most Ukrainian churches.

Light Switch: Worldliness vs. Holiness

The example of the Confessing Church in Germany, as well as the many believers throughout the history of Christianity who have remained faithful under persecution, are both an example and an encouragement to us. As Jesus promised, even death itself will not overcome the church and so the light of the church cannot be extinguished by its enemies. Yet the church has access to its light switch. Jesus warned his disciples not to switch it off by putting the lamp under a bowl. The lamp without light becomes a part of the surrounding darkness. It is an image of the church switched to the "worldliness" mode and therefore cannot be distinguished from any other social institution by an outsider. It could decorate itself and pretend that it has the light, but it is not the holy light of the kingdom of God.

There are many aspects and details in the appearance and liturgy of the Russian Orthodox Church that convey the idea of holiness. Its churches and monasteries often have golden domes shining dazzlingly in the sun, its priests make splashes of holy water glistening in the glow of numerous lamps. It uses many shining candles, the brilliant finery of the priests, icons with golden frames, images of the saints with golden shining halos around their faces. All these images of light, accompanied by the beautiful songs of the choir and surrounded by smoking incense, give visitors impressions of holiness. The Church's purpose is to give people a foretaste of the future kingdom of God and suggest that the Church is the kingdom of God's representation on earth. However, these signs can be misleading if they do not correspond to the inner essence of Christ's holiness. Once the contradiction between the external and the internal is discovered, the external becomes the symbol of fakery and lies.

One of my favourite Christian songs during the time of persecution in the USSR was dedicated to the light of truth shining through the storms of evil:

> . . . The storms of evil could not extinguish
> [the holy heavenly flame],
> While through the fires of trial
> The grey-haired elders carried it . . .
> We will take the banners of Christ's teaching
> From their weakening hands
> And . . . will carry the light of truth into the darkness.[36]

---

36. Yakov Buzynnyi, "Ныне Божья любовь обнимает (*Nyne Bozhia lubov obnimayet*: [God's love embraces now])," no. 716 in "*Песнь Возрождения* (*Pesn' Vozrozhdenia*: '*Song of Rebirth*')" (Soviet Union: Council of Churches of Evangelical Christians-Baptists, 1978), 461;

However, the forces of evil try to extinguish the holy flame not only by violent storms of persecution, but also by counterfeiting the refreshing breath of beauty and goodness. The tricks of the Antichrist are insidious and dangerous. He has mastered the art of presenting himself as an angel of light.[37]

Lamps for Lenin	**Light Against Darkness**	**Women, break religious shackle**

The rulers in the atheist Soviet Union understood well the power of the light metaphor. Their antireligious posters, especially in the early years of the Soviet regime, showed the church as the place of darkness and fakery, while the Soviet society was depicted as the kingdom of light and truth.[38] One of the tools of Soviet propaganda was the myth of the "Ilyich lamp," which was supposed to remind citizens of Vladimir Ilyich Lenin's promise that the entire country would be "flooded with light."[39] A famous Leninist slogan in the USSR was "Communism is Soviet power plus electrification of the entire country." For the followers of Lenin, the Communist Party was the light of the world

---

my translation of the Russian. "God's love embraces now" is the name of the hymn and *Song of Rebirth* is the name of the hymnal.

37. 2 Corinthians 11:14–15.

38. The first poster is "Little Lamps for Lenin." Lenin is depicted as the Light(bulb) of the World. https://thelittleredblog.typepad.com/blog/2021/06/little-lamps-for-lenin-part-four.html.

The second is "LIGHT against DARKNESS. The bright yellow and red of the full colour version are striking. Soviet modernity is the light, and darkness is only found in the shadow of the church. https://novosti-n.org/ukraine/Plakati-yz-knygy-o-sovetskoj-antyrelygyoznoj-propagande-FOTO-242845.

The third poster is "Women, Break the Religious Shackles, Build Socialism." It depicts Christian church leaders as the source of superstition and darkness, and Soviet industry as light. https://vartalife.com.ua/uroky-istorii-napady-na-tserkvu-cherez-stolittia/.

39. According to a venerated myth, Lenin said these words while attending the launch of electric light in a small village near Moscow.

To make sure that the church was not able to compete with the Bolsheviks' new ambition to be the light of the world, the Soviet regime physically destroyed tens of thousands of churches, monasteries, and houses of prayer while many thousands of priests, pastors, and active Christians were executed, and even more were sent to GULAG.[40] The final blow to the church was attempting to afflict it from within by infiltrating false priests and pastors into the church, as well as by recruiting informers or new KGB agents among existing believers and leaders of Christian communities.

One day in the late 1970s I was travelling on a train. A much older man sitting next to me noticed that I was reading the Bible and struck up a conversation. He told me about his uncle who was an atheist and a member of the Communist Party. In the 1930s, his party assignment was to study the Bible at an Orthodox seminary so that he could become a priest. After graduating from the seminary and until his death, this man continued to serve in the church, reporting to the Party on what the believers were saying. "These are the people who teach the Bible you are reading now. You can't trust this book and this church," my fellow traveller concluded.

Thirty years later in newly independent Ukraine, I was riding on a train from Kyiv to Donetsk and sharing my faith in God with my fellow passengers. Among them was a young woman who responded by expressing her doubts based on her recent experience. She told me about her new acquaintance who was an agent of the "religion department" in the Security Service, one of the remnants of the KGB that still existed in post-Soviet Ukraine. "And so, I asked him," the woman continued, "who could he recommend as a devout Orthodox priest in Donetsk to whom I could entrust my confessions and who could give me pious advice when I needed it?" She said that her acquaintance replied that there were no pious priests in that part of the country, declaring that they were all fake, all former KGB agents. "The Church cannot be trusted," she concluded, reminding me of words I had heard long ago.

This is the second necessary condition for the church to be a light to the world: it must have a direct and uninterrupted connection with the source of light. Any state may decide to use the church for its purposes instead of being guided by the light it transmits. An authoritarian state like the atheist Soviet Union develops a special skill of exploiting the church for its own purposes,

---

40. "Gulag" is a Russian anacronym: **G**lavnoe **U**pravlenie ispravitel'no–trudovykh **Lagere**ĭ ("Chief Administration for Corrective Labour Camps").

using deception, threat, blackmail, and corruption.[41] As we saw earlier in the Barmen Declaration, the church cannot maintain its identity with its king and his kingdom by submitting to the ungodly orders of earthly rulers (Acts 4:19; Matt 6:24). The problem with the church's accommodation to the state is that it then becomes one more obstacle obstructing the world in trusting the word of God and seeing its truth. Instead of being a light to the world, it helps the enemy of God to spread darkness.

The "storms of evil" have different guises. Today, in Russia, in the third year of its full-scale invasion of Ukraine, the price for speaking out against the Kremlin's lies and the crimes of its army is very high. I am grateful to those few Christians in Russia who are willing to pay this price. Silence in such circumstances can hardly help society see the light of truth when it is blinded by the power and lies of its dictator. What is absolutely shocking, however, is that many Christian believers, including pastors and church leaders in the Russian Federation, are willing to openly support Putin's regime. They remind me of the "German Christians" of the 1930s who followed the worldly charisma of their *Führer*.

With new technologies and new opportunities to manipulate and control large groups of believers, the forces of evil have even easier ways to divide the church. Many believers in the world today believe that a tool for fulfilling their mission is in the hands of a strong political leader who promises the world some kind of salvation. I am writing these pages in February 2024, a few days after a former prime-time Fox News host, Tucker Carlson, interviewed Russian president-dictator Putin about the current war in Ukraine. Carlson has been known in recent years for being sympathetic to Putin, so the interview became effectively a platform for Russian propaganda. Christian faith and the church were several times in the centre of Putin's talk about historical reasons for starting the war. One of them was linked to the role of the church in the history of Russia. The unity of Ukraine and Russia, according to Putin, must be enforced by any means because it was based historically on common Orthodox Christianity. Russian culture, said Putin, is spiritual, unlike pragmatic Western society.[42]

---

41. Pursuing a policy of isolating the church from society, the Soviet state often played puppeteer with religious organizations, expanding its power by gaining the support of believers abroad and in international organizations at various peace forums.

42. When Carlson asked Putin if he sees "God at work" or "forces that are not human," Putin's answer was "To be honest, no, I don't think [that there is God who acts in our world]." He then expressed conviction that societies always develop according to fixed laws.

It seems this Christian nationalism attracts many Russian believers today. First, they are attracted to populist propaganda about Russian Christian spirituality, culture, and historical destiny, which makes Russians a special and privileged people among godless and pragmatic Western societies. They then accept the idea that Putin is an instrument in the hands of God to fight secular godlessness. They become deaf to the testimonies of Ukrainian believers who witness the genocidal actions of the Russian army on Ukrainian soil. Considering themselves first and foremost as *Russian* Christians, they tear themselves away from their identity with Jesus Christ, the centre and inner circle of the church's existence. Needless to say, the tragedy of the church substituting the identity of the kingdom of God for national identity does not exist only in Russia; it is also occurring elsewhere.

The switch from holiness to worldliness happens imperceptibly. The church domes continue to shine, the candles on the iconostases burn, words from the Bible are capitalized, spiritual values are proclaimed in television interviews and in the squares, but the light no longer reflects reality. It no longer comes from the source of true light. This means that darkness is coming.

Living in Tension

The church often feels the tension of staying in the middle between the corrupted and the holy, the secular and the eternal. Perhaps today it is especially difficult for the church to maintain its identity as being within the kingdom of God when many believers are attracted to temporary ideologies through social media, by the magnetic force of populist political slogans, or the belief that the main role of the church is to be one of the national institutions and political players.

How can the church be *holy*, intricately connected to its source of light, the kingdom of God, and at the same time *missionary*, not standing apart from the world around it, even when the secular society is rapidly polarizing in its opinions about what is good and what is evil? To find the answer to this question will mean that in the presence of various cultural, political, and military confrontations and conflicts, we must restore certain principles of attitude and judgment that lead to actions that are defined by our kingdom identity. And so, we can hope that our belonging to the kingdom of God makes us better citizens and members of society, a light to the world.

A good place to start is to ponder how different communities (including various secular communities and the church) form their convictions on some of the issues that are important to them. We could get help from

Oliver O'Donovan's 2001 Stob lectures "Common Objects of Love"[43] in which he discusses what unites people in their commitment to common actions. O'Donovan takes a lead from Augustine of Hippo's definition of a people as "a gathered multitude of rational beings united by agreeing to share the things they love."[44] He argues that "the better the things we love, the better we as the people" remind ourselves that the strong opinions that steer us towards actions are connected with our affections. It is "by sharing a common view of the good, we become . . . a 'people,' capable of common action, susceptible to common suffering, participating in a common identity."[45]

In *The City of God*, Augustine wrote about "two cities" or two ultimate communities that are defined by what they love and what they reject: "love of God to the point of contempt of self, love of self to the point of contempt of God."[46] The church's identity with the kingdom of God is real when its members are drawn to God, rejoicing in his presence and seeing everything in the world as good or evil in relation to him as their Creator. The secular communities find their identities in their representative objects, persons, histories, and ideas, which help them see the world through common lenses and living in it.[47] Yet, they cannot flourish apart from God's love as all other objects of love are simply counterfeits of the reality. In a temporal ("secular") state of things, they must humbly recognize that their worldview has its limits and that their common objects of love are less than perfect. When members of any society use their particular social experience to claim that their knowledge of the world and history is universal, they become guilty of the sin of idolatry.[48] O'Donovan concludes that, while different societies have different perspectives on the world, we must remember that it is God who created plurality and we must wait for the time when he reveals to us the whole picture.[49]

To live peacefully and in harmony, societies and nations of the world need to cross the barriers between them. To do so, they first need to find and accept

---

43. O'Donovan, Oliver. *Common Objects of Love: Moral Reflection and the Shaping of Community*. Grand Rapids: Eerdmans, 2002.

44. Augustine, *City of God* 19.24. Amended definition from Cicero who used "law and common interest" instead of "the things they love." See O'Donovan, *Common Objects of Love*, 21. This love is not the love of 1 Corinthians 13, but it is "undetermined with respect to its moral quality," O'Donovan, *Common Objects of Love*, 22.

45. O'Donovan, *Common Objects of Love*, 21–22.

46. Augustine, *City of God* 19.28. Cf Matthew 22:37–38.

47. O'Donovan, *Common Objects of Love*, 31–36.

48. O'Donovan, *Common Objects of Love*, 41.

49. Genesis 3:1–7 and 11:1–9.

a universal overarching society, which is disclosed to them as the kingdom of Heaven. It gives a new identity to those who become members of the community of Jesus Christ, "our double representative, very God and very man."[50] The goal of the Antichrist is to give societies a false universal, which entices societies with images of power (authoritarianism), illusions of legitimacy (naïve populism), and manipulated stereotypes (mass media).[51]

Finally, O'Donovan makes references to two reminders from the Apostle John about how the church should resist the false universals of the Antichrist and show the power of its own objects of love. The church needs to be alert, as it might be stripped of its true identity and instead be represented "by the alien image" (Rev 16:15). It also needs to be patient when it goes through conflict (Rev 14:12).[52] It will find strength in focusing on the ultimate object of love, its true representative, and worshipping him.

The question of how we can live in the tension between being relevant to the temporal and faithful to the eternal brings us to the question of what really inspires us and what we worship in our daily lives. A puzzling hint that Jesus gave when explaining the metaphor of light to his followers can help us better understand his vision of the church shining with the light of his glory. What indeed is that city built on a hill that cannot be hidden? Some American Christians today claim that it might be the USA with its Christian heritage, some Russian Christians would argue that it is Moscow with its Orthodox culture.

Jesus, of course, spoke about an image familiar to his listeners. The most obvious exhibit of the "city on the hill" for his Galilean listeners was Sepphoris, a city located about six kilometres northwest from Nazareth. Herod Antipas called it "Autocratoris" and turned it into what the Jewish historian, Flavius Josephus, once described as "the ornament of the Galilee." Josephus wrote that, at sunrise, Sepphoris would light up the sky. Bryan Widbin, Professor Emeritus of Hebrew Bible at Alliance Theological Seminary, explains:

> Its *meleke*-limestone could take your breath away. But Jesus has something else in mind. He says to those who would listen, "Let *your* light shine before others that they may see the *good that you do.*" You want to know what that looks like? Look at Jesus in the

---

50. O'Donovan, *Common Objects of Love*, 44.

51. O'Donovan, *Common Objects of Love*, 66–67.

52. O'Donovan, *Common Objects of Love*, 71.

upper room. Draped in the towel of a servant, crawling around on his hands and knees, washing the feet of his dinner guests.[53]

If we ever were attracted by the humble heart of the One whose glory fills the whole earth, and yet whose title was "Servant," if we ever were humbled, realizing that he, so distinct from this world with his superlative holiness, still invites us to follow him and do things as he has done, if we ever were affected by the beauty of serving others instead of caring for our own reputation, then we can see the difference between the deceitful light of Sepphoris and the true light of the "city that does not need the sun or the moon to shine on it, for the glory of God gives it light, and the Lamb is its lamp."[54] The nations need to see the reflection of this light today so that one day they may walk by its light.

---

53. R. Bryan Widbin, "Dress for Success," Sermon on Matthew 5:13–16, given as an address delivered on the occasion of the thirteenth anniversary of International Christian Fellowship Church in Suffern, New York, USA, on 24 September 2023.

54. Revelation 21:23.

7

Body and the Church

Wojciech Szczerba

Body: Postcards from the Edge

Let me start with a few personal notes, a type of *Postcards from the Edge*.[1] The birth of my children. What a moment in life! It happened years ago, but still, when I am going back in my memory to this very moment, it always gives me shivers. I remember very well the second when I took my just-born daughter into my arms. I simply could not believe it was happening, it was absolutely beyond me. The little baby, the tiny body in my arms. One could say that nothing special had happened, just a circle of life. And the infant? Wrinkled, still with some blood and body fluids on her, an umbilical cord hanging, reddish skin, disproportionately big head, and very loud. Yet, for me, the world stopped instantly. This was the moment of epiphany, a pure miracle, God speaking to me. Naïvely, I thought I knew what was going to happen. I was totally wrong. I had no idea; the reality totally outgrew my imagination. The tiny body I was holding in my arms was the most beautiful thing I had ever seen or touched. I was blind to all the flaws and imperfections. I saw the miracle of the beginning of life, and I was holding a perfect body in my hands.

When my son was born a number of years later, I thought I was prepared for the second shock. Far from the truth! I was not at all. Again, all the concepts of birth, evolution, and transmission of life disappeared in a second. The tiny perfect-ugly body in my arms made me speechless and powerless. The heaven opened and the cry of the tiny fellow was like the voice of the Universe. All the memories disappeared. It was happening again, but really again for the first time. A perfect body in my hands!

---

1. Referring to the title of Mike Nichols's movie from 1990.

I am looking at my kids now, at this very moment, when I am writing these very words. A teenager and grownup young lady. How did it happen? All these years passed in the blink of an eye. Still, for me, as a father, they are just babies, and – naturally, in my biased perception – they are perfect (except when they argue with me). Right now, I see them playing badminton in our backyard. Lots of fun, sarcastic jokes, some competition, and a lot of energy. Their bodies are beautiful, harmonious, and agile. Nothing is impossible! They are full of life and full of energy, too much of it. A sheer excess of life! If only I could immortalize this moment! Do they know that they are slowly entering a grownup, independent life and a world that is not always so friendly? Do they know that this is just a moment in history and will pass away so quickly?

And I am looking at myself, a middle-aged man, who just a moment ago, it seems, was only entering his grownup life. I still tend to think of myself as if I was twenty or thirty, but a quick look at my kids sobers me up. It is long gone. Physically, in my body, as my wife graciously admits, I am still ok but now – for some reason – it requires a lot of work. I am gullibly convincing myself that the gym, jogging, cycling, diet, and various cosmetics make me look younger than I actually am, accommodate somehow my thinking of myself to my *real* self, if there is anything like a *real self*. Does it, really? Perhaps, as Heidegger noticed decades ago, I can already feel the horizon of my existence and I am simply getting anxious. In my fear-*Angst* I am falling into a mythical world, as the German philosopher says, leaving aside the possibility of the authentic existence and pretending that there is no inevitable end. Am I like that, crawling back to my cave of safe, but really phantasmatic, realm? Well, but then, a quick look at my kids straightens me out again, and – to be honest – I feel a bit worn out with my grey hair, vision getting worse, a few scars, and – however hard it is to admit – not as flat a belly as it used to be. My body is not exactly as I remember it.

And then my parents, especially my father, who is just turning eighty. He is getting old and fragile and needs more and more help to get by. His health is not as good as it used to be. I look at his thin, grey hair, wrinkles on his face, flaccid, pale skin, slightly hunched posture, and – I have to admit it – I love it. He is beautiful, with a special type of beauty. His body is like a map to me. Looking at him I can see countless hours we spent together: tedious homework, common vacations, games, breakfasts and dinners. In spite of his demanding work, he somehow found time to teach me how to play chess, speak German and Russian, understand chemistry (never succeeded), or pray an evening prayer. He was not always very patient, I have to say, but now it somehow does not matter much. It was not always easy! I remember a traumatic moment at the beginning of the 1980s when the secret police suddenly visited us in the middle of the night and arrested my father. Being a publisher in a communist country was not that safe. It took a moment and a mere pretext to crush a person not subscribing to the orthodox policy of the regime. Several months later he was back with us, but it took years before he fully recovered. It was a painful, yet very important, experience for our family. So, now I look at my father and I see a book of life in his body. I can somehow read it, and I love it. I see a person, who went out of *Plato's cave* to experience freedom in communist Poland, and then, as a free person, he came back to teach me how to live a free life. He is getting old and fragile now, but his body is a beautiful map to me and a mirror in which I can see myself.

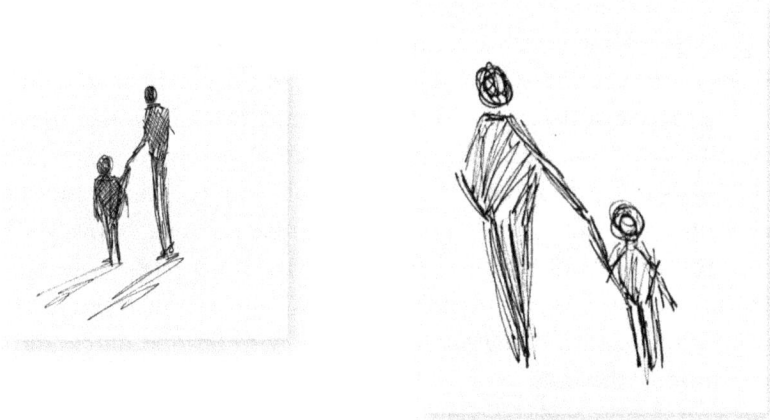

These are a few thoughts, just a couple of postcards from the edge, which immediately come to my mind when I think of the body in its metaphorical sense. There are naturally a few other pictures, which I have in mind as well. Here is a good friend of mine in a wheelchair, whose body does not function very well. He cannot move without help; he cannot live an independent life. Yet, it is he who teaches me about freedom and shows how to take care of others. He showed me how to read the symbolic painting of Chagall, so beautifully expressing the desires and pains of his soul. He also convinced me that we all are disabled, it is just a matter of time until we realize that. His body, through the example of his life, even though so fragile and imperfect is a beautiful symbol of being-for-others, as Bonhoeffer used to say in Tegel prison of Berlin.

And then, there was a student of mine, who died of cancer a few years ago. I remember visiting him in a hospital before he passed away. His disfigured body was difficult to accept. His suffering and his pain; I couldn't take it. It seemed so unfair. I would do anything to help him. And he was simply dying in agony. But then I saw him, in his pain and disfigurement, serving others in the hospital. He simply helped them as much as he could, he told them of his hope in Christ and shared his love in a very simple way. While dying in pain, he was fully present to others. I saw people leaving the oncology ward changed, with hope in their hearts, dying, yet not in despair but with hope. I am thinking of this student of mine now and his body changed by the horrible disease. It looked horrifying but it brought so much beauty to other people's lives. His face and his body became a metaphor for hope and love for me.

From this perspective, I look at the disfigured statue of Christ, which I regularly see in Malta. It is startling, barely recognizable, and disfigured by the wind and water. It always makes me stop and think of Christ in this world. It makes me wonder about his presence–absence in my reality. Is he like my father, getting old but beautiful in his old age, with his scars and wounds? Are they signs of his centuries-long ministry to the people, his commitment to the human race regardless of how much we hurt him? Is he like the student of mine, sick and disfigured with all the human blows and diseases falling on him? Yet, with a close look, can one see the real beauty of Christ and sense his lifegiving ministry still offered to humankind? Or perhaps – however heretical it sounds – is Christ simply fading away in this world, in the so-called Western hemisphere, in my world? There has been so much filth associated with institutionalized Christianity in my country, in Europe, and in the world. So many moral problems, so many financial scandals, so much depravation of those who should lead the community and call themselves representatives of Christ on the earth. Is he fading away? Is the statue of him, of his body, a symbol, a metaphor for his disappearance?

Sculpture of Christ, Valetta, Malta
Photograph by Author

Body: The Metaphor through the Ages

One of the basic, universal experiences of humanity is *being in the body* or simply *embodiment*. This is how we exist, this is how we perceive reality, this is – in a sense – who we are in our temporal, earthly presence. The body, "the whole physical structure that forms a person,"[2] is the primary source of knowledge about the self, society, and the world. Existing in a body is a fundamental experience of every person, regardless of age, gender, race, or culture. There is no other way of existence in this spatiotemporal world; the body somehow marks the earthly pilgrimage of every human being from their beginning to the end – birth to death. In various cultures and at various times the human body has been understood and conceptualized in diverse ways. However, its fundamental meaning as a physical structure of a person is the same and reflects the primary existential experience of all humanity.

---

2. "Body." Cambridge Dictionary, n.d., https://dictionary.cambridge.org/dictionary/english/body.

When thinking of conceptualizations of the human body in various cultures over the ages, a few simple observations can be made.[3] First, it is very natural to think of the human body in terms of gender; all cultures reflect sexual divisions in their projections of human physical structure. Simply, male and female bodies look different, men and women play distinctive social roles, especially in premodern societies, and participate in different cultural practices. Types of work, roles in families, places in social structures, and conceivable involvements in cultural activities are assigned differently in early or classical cultures for males and females. This is often reflected in different metaphorical projections of bodies of different sexes, especially since these conceptualizations were naturally influenced by certain religious beliefs, most of the time very patriarchal in their nature. Thus, even in medieval or early modern Christian Europe, female physical identity was often theologically perceived in terms of a lascivious, sinful, mortal, and irrational nature, whereas masculinity was connected with mind, immortality, and reason.[4] It is not a surprise that leading deities, celestial beings, or their earthly priestly representatives were typically – in premodern cultures – conceptualized as masculine, whereas womanhood was often associated with the fall and deprivation of the human race. It is biblical Eve who seduced Adam and not Adam who misled Eve into the original sin (1 Tim 2:13–14). The Western depiction of the human body based on sexes started to evolve in the Renaissance of the fifteenth and sixteenth centuries. Artists such as Da Vinci, Michelangelo, Raphael, Botticelli, and Tiziano (aka Titian) portrayed the human body as beautiful, referencing both males' and females' physicality. They returned to the ancient Greek concepts of an ideal, symmetrical body with harmonious proportions. Da Vinci's *Vitruvian Man* is a kind of icon or archetype of a synthesis of the scientific and artistic ideals of the human body of the High Renaissance, understood as a metaphor for the universe in a microcosm.[5] The studies of scientists and artists of the modern period evolved into the depiction of a generic body that was universal and

---

3. I am restricting myself here mainly to the so-called world of Western culture, which was significantly influenced by Greek–Roman culture and by biblical tradition, mainly Judeo–Christian.

4. Bitel, Lisa M. *Women in Early Medieval Europe 400–1100*. Cambridge: Cambridge University Press, 2002, esp. 13–46. Such misogyny was common in Roman and Hellenistic culture and philosophy, and was later imported into Christian cultural tradition, but this misogyny is not found in the pages of the New Testament.

5. Heydenreich, Ludwig Heinrich. "Leonardo da Vinci: Italian Artist, Engineer, and Scientist." In *Encyclopaedia Britannica*, 30 April 2024. https://www.britannica.com/biography/Leonardo-da-Vinci. Bambach, Carmen C. *Leonardo da Vinci Rediscovered*. Vol. 2: *The Maturing of a Genius: 1485–1506*. New Haven: Yale University Press, esp. 224.

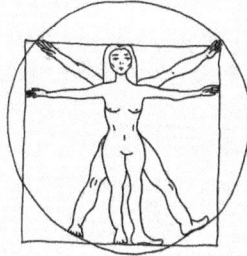

ungendered. Yet, in the following centuries, the male body was still depicted as a norm and the female physique as some kind of derivation from it, imperfect, and deprived of male organs.[6] This patriarchal understanding of humanity and human physicality was reflected in most areas of human existence and activity, including in language. Such phrases as "all men are equal in the eyes of the law," "evolution of man," "dignity of men," or "salvation of men" often served and many times still serve as general references to all people, male and female. Only the end of the nineteenth century and the twentieth century brought the general reconceptualization of sexes first on the wings of the process of equal rights and then the broadening of the spectrum of gender identity from binary to broadly understood nonbinary or transgender identities.[7] These processes of the evolution of the understanding of human sexuality and physicality are reflected nowadays more and more often in – at least some – languages, where we not only differentiate between basic descriptions of professions practiced by men and women for example, *businessman* and *businesswoman* or *postman* and *postwoman/mail lady*, but we also use various pronouns to reflect gender identity of a person in a way that upholds their understanding of themselves and their dignity.[8]

Second, in contrast to Eastern cultures permeated by monistic Taoism or Buddhism Zen, for example, Western culture, built predominantly on Hellenic and Judeo-Christian traditions, by and large perceives reality dualistically. It differentiates between body and soul/mind in the microscale of human beings, and typically between the immanent and transcendent (at least to

---

6. Following the Aristotelian perspective, for example, *Politics*, 1245b12, 1259a41, 1260a11.

7. I am here simply describing the cultural/social process of how societal understandings by sexes of their roles has changed over time.

8. In many parts of the world an increasing number of people are adopting identitarian ideologies and politics. This includes various gender identities that are not based in biological or ontological reality.

human perception) reality in the macroscale of the cosmos. Philosophical sources of such perception of reality can be traced to the old Orphic myth of Dionysius Zagreus, who is killed and eaten by the Titans.[9] They are trying to take revenge on Zeus, Dionysius's father, for throwing them into Hades. Unfortunately, Zeus is not able to save his son, but he kills and burns the Titans with his bolts of lightning. From the ashes he creates human beings, who in their composition consist by the necessity of the depraved titanic nature, but also the divine particle of Dionysius devoured by Titans. So, the myth teaches that humans are in their nature dualistic beings; their bodies are transient and mortal, and their souls/psyches are godlike and immortal. In fact, the soul is imprisoned in the body-*soma* as in the grave-*sema*, from which it has to free itself to return to its primal state, or – in other words – attain salvation. The myth was translated into the philosophical anthropology of Pythagoras and his students, and adopted by Plato.

Yet Plato's philosophy can be also traced to the tradition coming from other sides of Hellenic culture, namely the Homeric epics, maintaining the organic coexistence of body and soul. In the eleventh book of *The Odyssey*, Odysseus meets his late friend, Achilles, who comes to meet him from the land of the dead. The souls of the deceased are – as Homer maintains – blind as bats, without sensations, feelings, or perceptions. They are like zombies. A blood offering revives them and brings them back to consciousness for a short while. Yet it is a tragic moment, when they realize the misery of the disembodied life. As Achilles confesses, it is better to be "a beggar on earth than a prince in Hades." Death, separating body and soul, is for him the greatest evil.[10] Here is the paradox of life; according to Homer, a human being lives thanks to the soul and the soul is immortal. Yet, the life of a person is inevitably connected with being in the body. It gives sensations, feelings, memory, and (generally) consciousness to a person. The soul, pre-Socratic philosophers maintained, is a principle of life and rationality; it is differentiated from the body, yet as a splinter of the cosmic *arche*-principle it is substantial in its nature, as substantial

---

9. West, M. L. *The Orphic Poems*. Oxford: Clarendon Press, 1983, esp. 154–156; Ganz, Timothy. *Early Greek Myth: A Guide to Literary and Artistic Sources*. Baltimore: Johns Hopkins University Press, 1996, esp. 118–119.

10. Gajda-Krynicka, Janina. "Ciało i cielesność w filozofii starożytnej" [Polish: "The Body and Corporeality in Ancient Philosophy"]. Unpublished presentation, international conference on "Cielesność jako przedmiot refleksji w najnowszej filozofii" ["Carnality as an Object of Reflection in Recent Philosophy"]. Ustron, Poland, 12–14 May 2009, esp. 3. For a report on the conference proceedings, see Struzik, Elżbieta. "Cielesność jako przedmiot reflekcji w najnowszej filozofii" ["Corporeality as an object of reflection in recent philosophy"]. *Folia Philosophica* 28 (2010): 239–246.

as the body also built out of *arche*-principle. The soul constitutes the centre
of life, yet it is sustained and protected by the body. It actually makes humans
to be human; it is the basis of sensual life; and finally, it is an essential tool of
the soul of rational cognition.[11]

In the early and middle Platonic dialogues (e.g. *Apology, Symposium,
Phaedo, Phaedrus, Timaeus*), the philosopher believed that ideas constitute
the primary being and the soul somehow bounds a person with the realm of
ideas (*Phaedo, Phaedrus*). He believed – following the Orphic–Pythagorean
teaching – that it is important to cast away one's carnality with its sensual
existence. Instead, a person should take care of their soul and commit themselves to philosophy, which prepares a person for death and a happy existence
beyond the earthly, spatiotemporal life. Body-soma is just a grave-sema for
the soul-*psyche*, some kind of punishment for the original sin (*Phaedrus*) or
an effect of the law of necessity (*Timaeus*). However, in the later dialogues,
Plato changed his perspective on body and embodiment. In such dialogues as
Parmenides or *Philebus*, he moved beyond ideas in his attempt to find the
fundamental form of being. He asked questions about the model of existence
that leads to happiness (*Philebus*). In his search, Plato was not as strict as he
was in his early writings. He differentiated between sensual and contemplative
happiness. However, he did not elevate one at the cost of the other. He did not
defend any extreme. Rather, he believed that a happy life is linked with goodness, that is, with a specific combination of sensual pleasures and philosophical
contemplation. It is important to keep proper proportions and measures. On
the basis of this argumentation, Plato – following the pre-Socratic philosophers – believed that the human being is a kind of microcosm, an aggregate
of body and soul, where both soma and *psyche* are essential and equal in their
statuses. Just like in the cosmos, the human soul (the principle of life) and
body (the material aspect of the universe), by definition coexist in their eternal
life. Naturally, the ontological statuses of the soul and the body are different.
The human soul, for Plato, is unbegotten, everlasting, undivided, and inde-
structible. The body is complex, destructible, and begotten. Yet, both of these
principles constitute the *raison d'etre* of a human being, who is a mixture-*meixis*
of perishable and unperishable. As Plato adds in *Timaeus* (87c–d), one of his
last dialogues, the human body and soul, which ultimately come from the same
substance, have to be in proper balance, there needs to be a symmetry between
intellectual contemplation and sensual, physical urges. A person needs to take
care of the soul, but taking care of the soul means also caring for the body. A

11. Gajda-Krynicka, "The Body and Corporeality in Ancient Philosophy," 4.

person needs also to care for the body, but an integral aspect of that is also intellectual activity. "Only then a person will be called good and beautiful."[12]

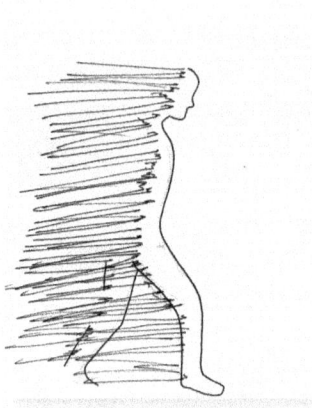

Plato's successors, including Aristotle and various philosophical schools of Hellenistic times, adopted and developed his views. They analyzed the onto-logical status, role, and function of the soul in its lifegiving and epistemological aspects. They also differentiated between the ontic statuses of the soul and the body. Yet, starting with the philosopher of Stagira, through Stoics, Epicureans, Cynics, Medio- and Neo- Platonists, they all appreciated the role of the body in the process of the realization of various functions and attaining the fate of the soul. Ultimately, the soul, regardless of the perceived dualism, belongs to the sphere of nature – physics, not metaphysics.[13]

Third, the body has been projected and conceptualized in numerous ways over the centuries. It has been portrayed as an *animal* or *heavenly plant* (Plato). Orphic–Pythagorean philosophers imagined the body as a cage or a grave, in which the soul is confined; hence the wordplay: *soma* (body) – *sema* (grave). In medieval Christian thought the body – especially the body of a woman – is often believed to be a container of lust and sinful emotions. Yet, some church fathers associated particular aspects of the human body with *imago Dei*. Gregory of Nyssa believed that the upright position, opposable thumbs, and a mouth that is used not only for eating or fighting but also speaking, indicate

---

12. Aristotle, *Physics* 1.1.402a; Gajda-Krynicka, "The Body and Corporeality in Ancient Philosophy," 12.

13. Gajda-Krynicka, "The Body and Corporeality in Ancient Philosophy," 12.

the aspects of the image and likeness of a person to God.[14] Several centuries later, Descartes imagined the body as a complex machine, whose physiological functions can be explained by mechanical processes and movements of the bodily parts. Nowadays, the body is conceptualized at times as a computer with the brain as a CPU or as a communication network, where various parts of the body communicate effectively with the headquarters – the mind – through the nervous and endocrine systems.

At the same time, the body itself has served as a metaphor for various aspects of reality over the centuries. Stoics thinkers saw the cosmos at large as an organized body with Logos at its centre. Neoplatonic philosophy, on the other hand, referred to humanity en bloc in terms of one body or one person. When adapted to Christian tradition, the Cappadocian fathers of the fourth century, and especially Gregory of Nyssa, pointed out that the name "human being" in a proper sense refers to all humanity and customarily only individuals are called human beings. According to him, just as there is only one God, but we believe in the Father, the Son, and the Holy Spirit, so – analogously – there is one human being, that is, the whole of humanity, of which individuals are mere exemplifications. Moreover, just as one body is interrelated and coherent, individuals in one human nature/person are interrelated and should live in solidarity. From this perspective, Gregory of Nyssa maintained in his famous fourth homily on Ecclesiastes, slavery is unacceptable as de facto "hurting ourselves," and helping the poor is an obligation for everybody. It is really a way of upholding the one body of humanity.[15]

On a smaller scale, a state, nation, or city was portrayed as one body many times in history.[16] Plato,[17] Aristotle,[18] Dio Chrysostom,[19] Plutarch,[20] Josephus,[21] or Philo[22] often refer in their writings to their societies in terms of a body, in

14. Szczerba, Wojciech. "The Concept of Imago Dei as a Symbol of Religious Inclusion and Human Dignity." *Forum Philosophicum* 25, no. 1 (2020): 13–36, 24. https://doi.org/10.35765/forphil.2020.2501.2.

15. Szczerba, "The Concept of Imago Dei," 27.

16. McVay, John K. "The Human Body as Social and Political Metaphor in Stoic Literature and Early Christian Writers." *The Bulletin of the American Society of Papyrologists* 37, no. 1/4 (2000): 135–147.

17. Plato, *The Republic*, 5.464B.

18. Aristotle, *Politics*, 1.1–2.

19. Dio Chrysostom, *Disc.*, 17; 33.

20. Plutarch, *Vit. Sol.*, 18.88.131.

21. Josephus, *J.W.* 4, 406–407.

22. Philo, *Spec. Leg.*, 3.131.

which all members should cooperate toward the common good, build strong family relationships as a basis for the healthy life of the body-society, obey the law, and be merciful toward fallen members of the society, who nevertheless are still parts of the one social organism. Various classes of society in this symbolism reflect the human body composed of various parts. They do not have to resemble each other, they may play dissimilar roles, and they may have different statutes in the bodily hierarchy, but still, each of them "contributes some particular service to the common good"[23] and constitute the bodily harmony. The head in this metaphor symbolizes the seat of intellect, a container of thought, or simply leadership, and is often associated with God, Caesar, a king, a high priest, or some other kind of leader. He is the one who unites every group, every age, and every part of the nation as a single body.[24]

The head-emperor and the state-body depend on each other; the body needs the head to exist, the head (or the soul at times) needs the body to exercise its power.[25] The collective aspect of the body is of fundamental importance in the ancient world. The state constitutes the social organism of the emperor/king/high priest; at the same time, every person is perceived and perceives themselves not only as an individual but also, or most of all, as an integral part of the social body of the state, guild, faith community, and/or family. Modern societies may be much more democratic in their structures, but still, the metaphor of body applies to them on various levels, for example, in terms of: (1) perceiving particular institutions as interrelated social organisms; (2) various roles of different classes of the society; (3) the law establishing the basic rules of coexistence; (4) the common good, for which all citizens should work; (5) the societal hierarchical ladder, conditioning public interdependences; or (6) the general spirit-pneuma permeating and binding together the social organism. The same metaphor of the body can be easily applied to other social groups like families, clubs, associations, companies, or churches.

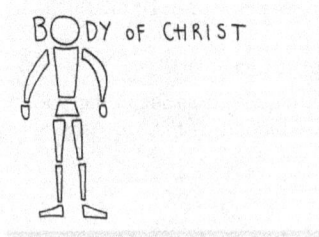

BODY OF CHRIST

---

23. Dionysius of Halicarnassus, *Ant. Rom.*, 6.86.3–4.
24. Philo, *Spec. Leg.* 3.
25. Seneca, *De Clementia*, 1.4.

Body: The Metaphor in the Pauline Epistles

The Apostle Paul in his letters many times refers to the metaphor of the body, mainly with the reference to the church, in its local or general dimension. In the metaphor, the head of the body is ascribed to Christ and the rest of the organism consists of Christians of the local community or Christians in general if the general aspect of the church is referred to. The Apostle Paul does not write a lot about the earthly life of Christ. Paul refers to Jesus coming from the lineage of David, that he lived a faithful life, unjustly suffered at the hand of people, died on the cross, was resurrected, and finally physically ascended to heaven (Phil 2:5–11). Beyond that, there is not much revealed about who Jesus from Nazareth was in his temporal existence. Perhaps this is because Paul did not know the earthly Jesus as his first recorded meeting with Messiah was the epiphany on the road to Damascus (Acts 9). At that very moment, he experienced the resurrected Lord, the heavenly being, who had the power to change the course of things on the earth and certainly had the power to change the way of life of Saul of Tarsus.

It is not surprising then that in the Pauline epistles Christ is so often portrayed symbolically as the head of new humanity or as the second Adam who diverts the consequences of the fall for the whole human race (Rom 5:12–21). In the metaphoric language of Paul, Christ becomes some kind of cosmic entity or sphere in which (*en Christo*) (metaphorically, from above down) evil powers are destroyed by God, all sins of humanity are wiped out, human debts to God are paid, all believers are gathered, and (from below up) all Christians exist and participate in Jesus's death, resurrection, and glory. The body of Christ, disfigured, humiliated, and destroyed, a price for condemned humanity (in the language of Anselm of Canterbury in his *Cur Deus Homo*) encompasses all the believers, the church (Eph 2:16; Col 1:24). One loaf of bread broken in the Eucharist symbolizes somehow the union of the church with the broken body of Christ, who is the head of the church (1 Cor 10:15). At the same time the church, in an ontological sense, already participates in the resurrected body of Christ and his cosmic glory. However, epistemologically, it will be fully experienced only in the eschatological future (Rom 8). The vertical symbolism of God perceiving and partaking in humanity through Christ (*metousia*) and humanity participating in the death, resurrection, and glory of Christ (*parousia*) is translated then into a horizontal symbolism of interdependence of believers and their solidarity in the body of Christ, the church. Here, Christians are treated metaphorically as members of one another and of Christ, as they constitute the body of Christ, the ecclesia. Their mutual relationship is portrayed as being as close as the intimate relationship of husband and wife. Christ as the head is the one who plays the fundamental role in the body and at the same time he is the ruler over the body (e.g. Eph 1:22; Col 2:10; 1 Cor 11:3; 12:21).

The metaphor of the body evolves in Pauline epistles. In earlier letters such as 1 Corinthians or Romans, Paul refers mainly to local communities, as he is dealing with particular communal issues.[26] In the community of Corinth, it may be moral problems and various inner divisions, whereas in the case of the church of Rome, Paul is preparing the community for his first visit there. In both cases, the apostle is trying to convince the addressees that the Christian community, however diverse with various "spiritual gifts" it is (1 Cor 12), has to be united and cohesive. Just as in an organism there are various members, playing various roles and functioning in diverse ways, all of them are needed and all of them form one, well-integrated body (1 Cor 12:20). Paul repeats this motif in Romans that just as

> in one body there are many members and not all of them have the same function, so we, who are many, are one body of Christ, and individually we are members of one another. We have gifts that differ according to the grace given to us: prophecy, in proportion to faith; ministry, in ministering; the teacher, in teaching; the exhorter, in exhortation; the giver, in generosity; the leader, in diligence; the compassionate, in cheerfulness. (Rom 12:4–8, NRSV)

The local community is conceptualized as one body, and precisely one body of Christ. All the members are needed regardless of their roles, functions, and gifts. They have to take care of each other if the body is to be harmonious and well-integrated. There are no more important members and no less important members. Even the head is not distinguished from the rest of the body, it is a part of the whole organism, analogously to the other members. So, just like "The eye cannot say to the hand 'I have no need of you,' . . . the head [cannot say] to the feet, 'I have no need of you'" (1 Cor 12:21).

Yet in the later Pauline epistles, such as Colossians or Ephesians, the author broadens the metaphor, so it does not refer only to local churches anymore but to the Christian community en bloc.[27] The body as a metaphor for the church at large includes all the believers, not only members of local communities. However, from this general perspective, the church as in the case

---

26. McVay, "The Human Body as Social and Political Metaphor," 141; Martin, Dale B. *The Corinthian Body.* New Haven: Yale University Press, 1999, esp. 38–68.

27. Wall, Robert W. "Introduction to Epistolary Literature," *New Interpreter's Bible.* Vol. 10, edited by Leander E. Keck. Nashville: Abingdon, 2002, 373–380.

of the body, becomes not only a unified organism, but also a hierarchical structure, where the head – Christ – executes his authority over the whole body, and other parts of the bodily system manage their particular areas and responsibilities. Apostles, prophets, evangelists, pastors, and teachers refer to the offices of leadership and power. Their responsibility is to lead the body, the early growing Christian church, to a unity of faith and to maturity, both in terms of spiritual knowledge and morality. In this process, every person has their place and function and should be faithful to the assigned role, so the only fledgling ecclesia becomes in time a full or mature man (*eis andra teleion*). The process of growing is envisioned by the author as nurtured by common love-*agape*, which is marked on the one hand by grace, kindness, and on the other hand by responsibility, respect, and submission. It should lead to peaceful cooperation and in effect (*telos*) to the maturity of the whole body (Eph 4:11–16). The hierarchical undertone of the metaphor is developed in interpretations of the further part of the argument (Eph 5:21–33), where the church as a body is compared to the marital relationships between a man and a woman. For the author, Christ, as the head of the whole body-church, is an integral part of the body, yet he also rules over the body. The author finds an analogous situation in the spousal bonds of his time where on the one hand the husband and wife create a very close, intimate relationship – they become one body – yet, on the other hand, their relationship is very hierarchical, the wife is to be submissive to the husband and the husband exercises power over his wife as her head. The wife needs to fully obey her husband and the husband, as the one with the higher social status and power, needs to care for his wife with love, as she is part of his own household. Isn't it how Christ cared for the church, dying for it on the cross? Isn't it how the status of *pater familiae* was understood in ancient times?[28]

A similar aspect of hierarchy, power, and obedience in the context of the metaphor of body is seen in the letter to the Colossians (Col 1:24; 2:10; 2:18–19). The church is perceived here in general terms, as encompassing all believers of the young but growing Christian community. Christ is portrayed here again as a cosmic entity, the head over every authority and power in the world, as the fullness-*pleroma* of embodied deity, as the one who encompasses all the believers. In Christ, the author believes, is freedom; this is in opposition to "the world," which enslaves people. The church is the body which

---

28. This reflects upon an influential part of the reception history of Ephesians 5. Of course, such interpretations of Ephesians 5 completely miss Paul's radical subversion of Roman–Greco hierarchical and patriarchal assumptions – *the editors.*

must obey the head-Christ. It is the head which binds together the body in a proper way, gives it divine energy to grow, and leads it to maturity. The head keeps the whole body alive. The author – aware of the danger of diverging the young church from the original, apostolic faith – implies the highest authority of Christ who has risen and physically ascended to heaven over every other cosmological-mythical power. He wants – to put it straightforwardly – the addressees to accept all resources provided by the head to keep the unity of the body, that is, to accept his teaching as the one seconded by Christ.

This way of portraying the church at large resembles Greek and Roman references to the state as a body.[29] When Seneca, for example, in *De Clementia* (2.2) writes about Nero as the head of the state, whose kindness diffuses through *Imperium Romanum* and holds together the whole country, he uses very similar rhetoric: the whole image of the head and body; the kindness that comes from the head; the holding together of the body; giving it health; the expectation to be shaped into the likeness of the head. These are similar motifs used in various contexts in the ancient world. They refer to the universal experience of humanity being in the body. They also refer to the earlier literature and various rhetorical usages that were understood and accepted by the audiences of the Greek–Roman world.[30]

Paul's letters often refer to the metaphor of the body.[31] The metaphor serves as a conceptualization of the church as a local community in the earlier epistles or, in the later writings, as the church in general. It often indicates a vertical relationship when it refers to the union between the divine and human (Col 1:15–20; Eph 1:22–23) or dependencies between the head and the members of the body (Col 2:19; Eph 4:11–16). Yet, it also translates the vertical direction into the horizontal aspect of the metaphor and indicates the interrelationship of the members of the body, their coexistence, and also the need to cooperate and care for each other. Only in this way can the early Christian community, still in its neophyte stage, grow and mature in unity.

The aspect of love that encompasses kindness and compassion is predominant in the metaphor, especially in its earlier form, as the whole biblical salvation plan is based on divine love. Christ loves his body and in love keeps

---

29. See Dunn, James D. G. "The Body of Christ in Paul." In *Worship, Theology and Ministry in the Early Church: Essays in Honor of Ralph P. Martin*, edited by Michael J. Wilkins and Terence Paige, 146–162, Journal for the Study of the New Testament Supplement Series 87. Sheffield: JSOT Press, 1992.

30. McVay, "The Human Body as Social and Political Metaphor," 142.

31. Schweizer, R. Eduard. "Body." In *Anchor Bible Dictionary*. Vol. 1: A–C, edited by David Noel Freedman. New York: Doubleday, 1992, 767–772.

it together. All members of the body should also love each other and care for others, especially for those, who are weaker and somehow lower in the social scale of the body.

Yet, in the later forms of the metaphor, the aspect of hierarchy and power is added. It is not only love that diffuses through the body and keeps it together, but also a proper response to love, which is respect, obedience, responsibility, and acceptance of one's own and others' place in the body. This way the church becomes a power structure, first of all with the divine head ruling over all other powers, and then with various members of the body seconded by the head to play leadership roles within the body.[32] This is the way – according to Colossians or Ephesians – to keep the early church doctrinally safe, morally pure, and to have it grow in faithfulness to the early teaching of the apostles. The patriarchal model of the family with the strictly defined roles of the husband and wife in the Roman culture helps, it seems, to keep a proper balance between love, giving one's life for others, and respect, obeying the ones who take responsibility for the whole body or its aspects. (Paul consistently subverted Roman-Greek patriarchal expectations. Over time the church reverted to patriarchal cultural models, but it had to reinterpret Paul in order to do so.) This aspect of executing the power over the whole body-church would become predominant in the following centuries, with the development of Christian orthodoxy guarding the true faith, apostolic succession securing the power of the ones genealogically seconded by the apostles, the general centralization of the church in the Western and Eastern hemispheres, and the development of Christendom seeking to rule over the world and all the secular powers.

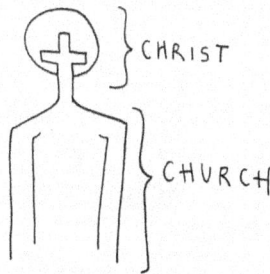

---

32. That is, under the power (*dynamos*) and authority (*exousia*) of Christ. Misappropriations of this concept, however, lead to abuse and should be avoided.

Body and the Church: Blessing or Curse?

Let me go back to the traumatic moment in the life of my family in 1983 when my father was arrested by the communist militia. They came to our house in the middle of the night, searched it thoroughly, and took my father away from us for long months. As a political prisoner, he was put in jail on the other side of Poland with common criminals. And not only that, they also took the savings my parents had, leaving my mother with just one small salary and two fast-growing teenagers. How did we survive? How was my mom able to provide for all of us? How were we able to visit my father every weekend, spending long nights on the train, to bring him food, warm clothes, books, and most of all our love and comfort? How was it possible? I tend to think of my mother as some kind of hero, which she absolutely was and still is to me. Yet, our survival would have been very difficult without the help of other people. Actually, it was the church that helped us at that time. We were regularly visited by the people from our Catholic community. They brought us food and clothes. Even now I remember the orange cheese and salty, American butter which we had at that time, olive oil from Italy, and canned tuna fish, such a rarity in late communist Poland. Similarly, notebooks, pencils, pens, and erasers for our schools were brought to us by priests and other people from the church. My mother was helped financially so that she could pay the bills and we would be able to visit our father. We experienced real love and comfort from our community, we did not feel lonely or abandoned. When I am going back in my memory to that period of life, I think we witnessed some kind of miracle which helped us survive in a very difficult time and circumstances. We saw God expressing God's love to us through other people. But perhaps it was not a miracle in terms of bypassing the laws of nature, but a very natural development of the vision of the church as one body set in the New Testament. This was just a small, but very vivid to us, example of how members of the body-church can extend their love and care for other members of the body-church. Whatever it was, it is still present in my memory and in my heart. I still feel very grateful.

I am sure that there have been countless cases of such examples of love and care shown within the church as one body over centuries in various parts of the world. Helping the poor, sick and needy, creating workplaces for the unemployed, establishing schools, developing good discipleship programmes, offering psychological support, granting scholarships, founding prison ministries, building houses, fighting natural disasters, and so on. Millions of Christians of various times, cultures, ethnicities, and genders have experienced the care of other Christians that they believe to be one body in Christ. This has been especially true in times of pandemics, wars, or natural disasters which somehow melt people's hearts and make them especially sensitive to the suffering of other Christians, members of the same body of Christ.

Yet, the church, as Dietrich Bonhoeffer dramatically points out in his *Letters and Papers from Prison*, "is the Church only when it exists for others . . . not dominating, but helping and serving. It must tell people of every calling what it means to live for Christ, to exist for others."[33] Is this how the church as the body of Christ has been functioning for centuries? Not dominating but helping and serving? Existing for others, those outside of the church, not ruling, not manipulating, not patronizing, and not taking care only of its own business and its own profit. I am sure there have been multitudes of examples of how the church in its local or general dimension has ministered to those who do not belong to the Christian community, whether Jews, Muslims, Buddhists, Hinduists, people of other religious views, or those who see themselves as agnostics and atheists. I am also sure that there have been countless cases of how the church served those who think otherwise in social, cultural, or moral matters, those who fall, or simply those who are different. I am sure the history of humanity is full of cases of the church serving the other. After the genocide in Rwanda, revolutions in northern Africa, wars in Syria, Ukraine, Sudan, and Myanmar, or so-called migration crises, a lot of help was organized from the church and distributed to those in need, regardless of their faith or religious adherence.

Yet, so many times in history the church, both in its general form and its local exemplifications, has been closed to those outside and has unscrupulously ruled over those inside, extending control, forgetting about love, and building political powers or exclusivist fortresses.[34] This exclusivism is often based on the assumption that a particular religion, denomination, or community is the faithful depositary of the spiritual truth revealed to humanity in a particular way (e.g. *Dominus Iesus* IV, 17).[35] Through exclusivist lenses, this ecclesia then grants itself the right to judge and influence the social order in which it exists. In the hands of ecclesiastical institutions, religious teaching naturally becomes a tool for initiating and strengthening the social divisions between "us" and "them," according to *extra Ecclesiam nulla salus* (no salvation outside of the church). Thus, the community of the *already saved* is naturally contrasted with

---

33. Dietrich Bonhoeffer, *Letters and Papers from Prison*, Enlarged Edition, edited by Eberhard Bethge. New York: Touchstone, 1997, 382–383.

34. Szczerba, "The Concept of Imago Dei," 17–18.

35. *Dominus Iesus* is a published statement of the Roman Catholic Church's Congregation for the Doctrine of the Faith. It is available in English at https://www.vatican.va/roman_curia/congregations/cfaith/documents/rc_con_cfaith_doc_20000806_dominus-iesus_en.html.

the community *outside of salvation*, the faithful "under the grace" compared with the unfaithful "outside of grace," "children of God" with the "children of the world," the City of God with the Earthly City. In the course of history, particular dogmas, doctrines, and theological structures have frequently served to strengthen the divisions between the chosen ones and the ones "of the world," sons of the church and the fallen ones (1 John 4:1–5). This type of strategy may be argued as a natural way to strengthen the identity of religious communities in which orthodoxy defines borders of the true faith. However, it is not unusual for ecclesiastical institutions of power to use a particularly understood set of beliefs to justify their existence in specific cultural contexts by translating religious truths into sociopolitical structures and authoritarian ways of executing their power. Extreme examples of such situations include persecution of pagans at the end of antiquity, medieval crusades, inquisition, religious wars, theological justification of slavery, fascism, Apartheid, sexism, antisemitism, or anti-Islamic movements.

Contemporary ecumenical and interreligious dialogue has been developing for more than 100 years, at least in the so-called "Western world." The work of the World Council of Churches (www.oikoumene.org/en) or the Lausanne Movement (www.lausanne.org) can serve as obvious examples. This ecumenical and interreligious dialogue has resulted in many positive outcomes. However, there are still challenges and barriers to this dialogue as a result of the doctrinal differences between confessions, the complicated and at times bloody history, or the particular policies of ecclesiastical, hierarchical institutions. This last example may be – paradoxically – the most difficult barrier to overcome. The church en bloc does not appear to be one, interrelated, cohesive body of Christ anymore.

I would like to finish my reflection on the church as a body (of Christ) with a personal note. Several years ago, I went with my children to an old Lutheran cemetery in the mountains. It was an amazing, breathtaking experience. Walking between the graves was like travelling through time. We could see tombs of Christians from several centuries ago. Some of them were destroyed by time, difficult even to notice. Yet, on many, we could read the stories of those who passed away a long time before we were born. We could read about their lives, families, beliefs, professions, and achievements. It was as if we would meet the witnesses of faith from the past and could listen to them. It was a beautiful experience! Between the graves, there was a statue of Christ. We had to stop when we noticed it.

It looked so natural – as if Christ stood between us. The statue was truly poignant and beautiful. Its whiteness among the grey tombs was astonishing. It attracted attention and it was difficult to look away from it, especially since Christ looked down, directly at us. Yet, the statue of Christ had no hands. What a drama, I thought! What a symbol! Perhaps Christ would like to hold a person and embrace them. Perhaps Christ would like to give a hand to somebody who is falling down. Perhaps he would like to pick up someone who is lying down and cannot move by themselves. Perhaps he would like to extend his love. But Christ has no hands. He seems to be helpless, so close to us, but separated from us by an abyss. His body is incomplete! He has no hands! What a drama, I thought!

And then I saw these two graves among some others in front of Christ. One of them belongs to Henryk Tomaszewski, an outstanding artist, a creator of the Polish school of pantomime, a hero for many, and a self-identified homosexual. Long before his death he joined the Lutheran community in this small town and asked to be buried in the graveyard. The other is the grave of a poet, Tadeusz Rozewicz, one of the best poets Poland has ever had. He lost his faith after witnessing the atrocities of WWII. As he writes in one of his poems: "I saw thousands of crippled bodies of people, who would never be saved," and then he adds that his faith disappeared like water sinking into the sand. One day he just woke up and it was gone. He became an atheist. But then several years before his death he met Bonhoeffer, as he says. Rozewicz read his writings and then wrote a beautiful poem "Learning to Walk," where he simply says that with Bonhoeffer he is learning how to walk again.

So, these two outstanding people are buried there now, in this Lutheran cemetery, in front of the statue of Christ, an atheist and self-identified homosexual. And the handless Christ is standing behind them, looking at them and, as it seems, smiling to them. The merciful Christ seems to be accepting all who come, no matter who they are. And then, looking at the graves of Tomaszewski and Rozewicz, I thought that perhaps in our twisted, complex world, people like them can serve as the hands of Christ. With their complicated stories, existential questions, deep doubts, challenges, and yet some kind of trust or hope, they show their human authenticity and the scope of the love of Christ. They simply demonstrate that everyone is welcome. Isn't it what the good news is about? This is what we learned with my children that day in this old Lutheran cemetery. Metaphors can grow old, change their meaning, and sometimes they die. Yet, the metaphor of the body of Christ may be still alive and significant as long as there are those who serve as his hands and point out to his unlimited love to the world.

> The Church is the Church
> only when it exists for others . . .
> not dominating, but helping and serving.
> It must tell people of every calling
> what it means
> to live for Christ, to exist for others.
> – Dietrich Bonhoeffer[36]

Body and the Church: So What?

The concept of the body constitutes a rich metaphor for the Christian community, the church. In a positive sense, it contains the notions of belonging to something greater than just our earthly, individualistic existence. It points out the interrelationship or solidarity of all believers that is based on the love of God. Isn't it God's love that lies at the heart of the work of creation and

---

36. Bonhoeffer, *Letters and Papers from Prison*, 382–383.

then the history of salvation? The notion of the body as a description of the church also builds the identity of Christians. We are all members of the same organism. We are all important and we are all needed if the organism is to function properly. There are no parts that are useless or redundant. Every person plays a significant role as a member of the divine body, the ecclesia, or to put it differently, the divine body includes every believer in its functioning. The "vertical" love of Christ-the head translates into the "horizontal" love of the members of the body to each other and serves as a witness and invitation to those who are outside of the body.

At the same time, in a negative sense, the concept of the body with reference to the church may easily be used as a means of domination. In fact, it has been used many times in history as a tool of control and oppressive power. The hierarchy organically contained in the notion of the body may make some of its parts more important and some less important, some noble and some shameful. The masculine, traditional imagination of the body may constitute some kind of patriarchal domination within the ecclesiastical body. Isn't it the case many times even today? The "special status" of the members of the body may easily serve not as a witness and invitation to those outside but as a means of exaltation of those inside and the reason for contempt of the others. Can the fundamental concept of the unity of the body truly be functioning without the metaphysical notion of the universal church, with all the multitudes of denominations, with their spiritual leaders-heads, and their spiritual policies so often causing social conflicts and tensions? What is the church as the body today? What is the body of Christ at the beginning of the twenty-first century?

I have sketched my own understanding of the metaphor of the body with reference to the church. Yet, I understand that I am perceiving it from my peculiar, Polish-Catholic, post-communist perspective of somebody who is trained in philosophical theology. I am aware that my story of ecclesia constitutes only a small aspect of the whole meta story of the church as a body. Now, it is time to see other perspectives and understandings, broaden the horizons outlined in the chapter, and learn from each other. It would be wonderful to draw together a multifaceted picture of the church as a body for the twenty-first century. So, let me ask a few open questions.

For Reflection

- What basic associations come to your mind when you think of the metaphor of the body?
- What notions does the metaphor of the body concerning the church evoke in your cultural context?
  - What positive associations do you see?
  - What negative associations might be disturbing?
  - What do you think are the church's prospects for the twenty-first century? Why?
  - What dangers do you see for the church in the twenty-first century?
- Can you tell your own story or the story from your cultural context in a manner that personalizes the metaphor of the body with reference to the church in its local or broader sense?
- What does it mean for you that the church is the body (of Christ)?
- How do you understand the thought of Dietrich Bonhoeffer in your own context: "The Church is the Church only when it exists for others . . . not dominating, but helping and serving. It must tell people of every calling what it means to live for Christ, to exist for others?"

Contributors

Antonio Carlos Barro
Brazilian pastor, writer, and theological educator, Antonio is the co-founder of South American Theological Seminary in Londrina, Brazil, where he serves as Professor of Missiology and Pastoral Theology. He earned a PhD in Intercultural Studies at Fuller Theological Seminary.

Jorge Henrique Barro
Born in Brazil, Jorge earned his PhD in Intercultural Studies at Fuller Theological Seminary. He is the co-founder and CEO at South American Theological Seminary, Londrina, Brazil, a former president of the Latin American Theological Fellowship (FTL), and an Evaluator for the Ministry Education of Brazil for Theology Degrees. A Presbyterian pastor, he has authored books in the fields of Missiology and Pastoral Ministry. Personal webpage: www.missaourbana.com.br

Oscar Jiménez
A Colombian New Testament scholar, Oscar earned his PhD in New Testament at London School of Theology. His doctoral thesis, "The Metaphors in the Narrative of Ephesians 2:11–22," published by Brill, has influenced masters and doctoral students in the field. Oscar serves as pastor in a Hispanic church in London and is an associate lecturer at Fundación Universitaria Seminario Bíblico de Colombia. His research focuses on bridging the gap between academia and the church and he aims to make his writings relevant and applicable to the church. He has authored a variety of books in both Spanish and English, ranging from popular to academic works. Oscar is married to Julieth Serna, and they have two children, Martina and Mathias.

John Jusu
A native of Sierra Leone, Dr. Jusu is a missionary with the Association of Evangelicals in Africa, seconded to Africa International University in Nairobi, Kenya. He is an ordained minister of the Church of the United Brethren in Christ, Sierra Leone. He is currently on an extended leave of absence from the university and is serving with Mesa Global as a Theological Education Consultant in Anglophone Africa. He works extensively on transformational curriculum issues in response to the contexts in which formal and informal education happens in Africa. His expertise is in understanding the episte-

mological frameworks of Africans striving to go into pastoral and teaching ministries of the African church, and how that understanding may influence educational practices. John serves as a curriculum consultant for the More than a Mile Deep-Global, supervising editor for the *Africa Study Bible*, Senior Researcher for the Africa Leadership Study, and a member of the Global Associates for Transformational Education. John is also involved in faculty development for many educational initiatives in Africa. John is married to Tity. They have three children.

Mark Labberton

Mark Labberton served the last ten years as president of Fuller Theological Seminary. Before that he was on the faculty of Fuller for four years in the Lloyd John Ogilvie Chair of Preaching. For over forty years, Mark has been an ordained pastor in the Presbyterian Church (USA), with most of those years being spent in two different roles at the First Presbyterian church of Berkeley, California. Mark has graduated from Whitman College, Fuller Theological Seminary, and Cambridge University. Since his time as one of John Stott's study assistants in the late 1970s, he has been involved in global theological education, including being a co-founder of Scholar Leaders and chair of John Stott Ministries, now Langham Partnership U.S. He has authored a number of books including *The Dangerous Act of Worship: Living God's Call to Justice*, *The Dangerous Act of Loving Your Neighbor: Seeing Others Through the Eyes of Jesus*, *Still Evangelical?*, and *Called*; he has also authored many articles. Mark currently serves on the board of International Justice Mission (IJM). Mark is married to Janet Morrison Labberton and they have two adult sons.

Elizabeth Sendek

A native of Colombia, Elizabeth earned her MA in Biblical Studies at New College, Berkeley. She served for twenty-eight years at the Biblical Seminary (FUSBC) in different capacities: professor (1993–2009), Academic Vice-President (2007–2010), and President (2011–2021). Previously, Elizabeth served with the Colombian student ministry associated with the International Fellowship of Evangelical Students (IFES). She has devoted most of her life to nurture Christ followers to serve in the church and society. She is passionate about theological education that combines theology, education, and context. As a theological educator, she has lectured internationally and is an associate of Global Associates for Transformational Education (GATE). Elizabeth authored *Griego para Sancho* ["Greek for Sancho'], an introductory grammar of New Testament Greek for Spanish-speaking students, the commentary on the Gospel of John for the *Comentario Bíblico Contemporáneo*, notes on the same gospel for *The Justice Bible*, and has contributed to other publications on theological education and leadership. Elizabeth was a board member of the Latin America Mission (LAM), the Evangelical Association of Theological Education in Latin America (AETAL), and Theological Book Network. Currently she serves on the boards of Mesa Global (previously United World Mission) and reSource Leadership International. She is married to Donald.

Wojciech Szczerba

Wojciech earned degrees from Graduate Christian Theological Academy in Warsaw (1996) and Economic Academy in Wroclaw (1997) before studying abroad at Theological Seminary in Amsterdam, the Netherlands, and at Evangelische Theologische Faculteit in Heverlee-Leuven, Belgium. In 2000 he completed his PhD in Patristics at the University of Wroclaw. In 2009 he defended his second PhD (habilitation) in Ancient Philosophy at the same university. Wojciech has written two books on universal salvation (*apokatastasis*) in ancient philosophy and co-authored and edited several publications on philosophy and theology, including Polish editions of *City Center Church* by Timothy Keller and a biography of Karl Barth by Mark Galli. He is the author of numerous articles dealing with such issues as anthropology, soteriology, Protestant tradition, ancient philosophy, and philosophy of religion. Wojciech became Academic Dean of the Evangelical School of Theology in Wroclaw, Poland in 2002 and served in this position until he became the Rector/President in 2006. Additionally, Wojciech serves as editor-in-chief of the periodical *Theologica Wratislaviensia* (https://theologica.ewst.pl/) and secretary to the Council of Evangelical Union in Poland. He participates in various ecumenical initiatives and interreligious dialogues. In 2018, Wojciech received the Silver Cross of Merit from the President of Poland in recognition of his ministry to preserve the identity of religious and cultural minorities in Poland. Since 2019, Wojciech has been a senior research associate at Von Hügel Institute at St. Edmund's College, University of Cambridge (https://www.vhi.st-edmunds.cam.ac.uk/directory/szczerba). His wife is Magdalena; they have one daughter and one son.

Sergiy Tymchenko

A citizen of Ukraine, Sergiy Tymchenko grew up in Kyiv in a family that was part of the underground Baptist church movement under the Soviet Union. He committed himself to the Lord when he was a student at the Moscow Power Engineering Institute. After being discipled by Navigator missionaries, he became involved in underground evangelism and discipleship networks. He began his ministry as a pastor of a church in 1985 and later received an MDiv from Denver Seminary and a PhD from the London School of Theology. He co-founded and was among the leadership of the mission society Light of the Gospel, the Center for Leadership Development, and the Association of Missionary Evangelical Churches of Ukraine. He also served as the chairman of CCX Ukraine, part of International Fellowship of Evangelical Students, and as a member of the IFES International Executive Committee. He founded and has been directing the Research Education and Light Center, known as REALIS, an interdisciplinary centre that trains Christian leaders and specialists and develops projects for strengthening the Christian witness to contemporary society. Hundreds of these leaders have received their MA in intercultural studies, sociopolitical ethics and theology, Christian counselling and chaplain ministry in crisis situations, and other programmes. Since the start of Russia's full-scale war against Ukraine in 2022, REALIS, under Sergiy's leadership, has been developing a number of humanitarian programmes, including a winterization project, construction of temporary housing, psychosocial support for children and adults, and a number of other activities.

Sergiy has taught at Donetsk Christian University, the North Caucasus Bible Institute, the Eastern European Seminary for the Education of Leaders, the National University of Kyiv-Mohyla Academy, Open Orthodox University of St. Sophia, and National Dragomanov Pedagogical University. He and his wife, Iryna, have two daughters and two sons and live in Kyiv, Ukraine.

Antonina Szczerba

Antonina is an emerging Polish artist and student at the University of Groningen, the Netherlands. With a deep passion for broadly understood art, she has developed drawing, film, photography, and fashion skills, bringing a unique perspective to each of her projects. While drawing remains her central passion, Antonina continuously explores new mediums and techniques and is always eager to expand her artistic horizons.

Langham
PARTNERSHIP

Langham Literature and its imprints are a ministry of Langham Partnership.

Langham Partnership is a global fellowship working in pursuit of the vision God entrusted to its founder John Stott –

> *to facilitate the growth of the church in maturity and Christ-likeness through raising the standards of biblical preaching and teaching.*

Our vision is to see churches in the Majority World equipped for mission and growing to maturity in Christ through the ministry of pastors and leaders who believe, teach and live by the word of God.

Our mission is to strengthen the ministry of the word of God through:
- nurturing national movements for biblical preaching
- fostering the creation and distribution of evangelical literature
- enhancing evangelical theological education

especially in countries where churches are under-resourced.

Our ministry

Langham Preaching partners with national leaders to nurture indigenous biblical preaching movements for pastors and lay preachers all around the world. With the support of a team of trainers from many countries, a multi-level programme of seminars provides practical training, and is followed by a programme for training local facilitators. Local preachers' groups and national and regional networks ensure continuity and ongoing development, seeking to build vigorous movements committed to Bible exposition.

Langham Literature provides Majority World preachers, scholars and seminary libraries with evangelical books and electronic resources through publishing and distribution, grants and discounts. The programme also fosters the creation of indigenous evangelical books in many languages, through writer's grants, strengthening local evangelical publishing houses, and investment in major regional literature projects, such as one volume Bible commentaries like *The Africa Bible Commentary* and *The South Asia Bible Commentary*.

Langham Scholars provides financial support for evangelical doctoral students from the Majority World so that, when they return home, they may train pastors and other Christian leaders with sound, biblical and theological teaching. This programme equips those who equip others. Langham Scholars also works in partnership with Majority World seminaries in strengthening evangelical theological education. A growing number of Langham Scholars study in high quality doctoral programmes in the Majority World itself. As well as teaching the next generation of pastors, graduated Langham Scholars exercise significant influence through their writing and leadership.

To learn more about Langham Partnership and the work we do visit **langham.org**

www.ingramcontent.com/pod-product-compliance
Lightning Source LLC
Chambersburg PA
CBHW072151090426
42740CB00012B/2223